Library of
Davidson College

CULTURE AND DEMOCRACY

Anthropological Reflections on Modern India

R. S. Khare
Department of Anthropology
University of Virginia

With a Preface by Kenneth W. Thompson

UNIVERSITY
PRESS OF
AMERICA

LANHAM • NEW YORK • LONDON

306.2
K45c

Copyright © 1985 by

University Press of America,™ Inc.

4720 Boston Way
Lanham, MD 20706

3 Henrietta Street
London WC2E 8LU England

All rights reserved

Printed in the United States of America

Co-published by arrangement with
The White Burkett Miller Center
of Public Affairs,
University of Virginia

Library of Congress Cataloging in Publication Data

Khare, R. S. (Ravindra S.)
  Culture and democracy.

  (American values projected abroad ; v. 14)
  Bibliography: p.
  Includes index.
  1. India—Politics and government—1947-
2. India—Social conditions—1947-   . 3. Democracy.
I. Title. II. Series.
JX1417.A74 1982   vol. 14   303.4'8273 s   84-29103
[JQ281]   [306'.2'0954]
ISBN 0-8191-4412-6 (alk. paper)
ISBN 0-8191-4413-4 (pbk. : alk. paper)

AMERICAN VALUES PROJECTED ABROAD

VOLUME XIV

A SERIES FUNDED BY THE EXXON EDUCATION FOUNDATION

FOUNDATIONS OF AMERICAN VALUES

Vol. I. Western Heritage and American Values: Law, Theology and History
By Alberto Coll

Vol. II Political Traditions and Contemporary Problems
Edited by Kenneth W. Thompson

Vol. III Institutions for Projecting American Values Abroad
Edited by Kenneth W. Thompson

Vol. IV Essays on Lincoln's Faith and Politics
By Hans J. Morgenthau and David Hein

Vol. V The Predicament of Human Rights: The Carter and Reagan Policies
By Nicolai N. Petro

Vol. VI Writing History and Making Policy: The Cold War, Vietnam, and Revisionism
By Richard A. Melanson

Vol. VII Traditions and Values: American Diplomacy, 1790 to 1865
Edited by Norman Graebner

Vol. VIII Traditions and Values: American Diplomacy, 1865 to 1945
Edited by Norman Graebner

Vol. IX Traditions and Values: American Diplomacy, 1945 to the Present
Edited by Kenneth W. Thompson

AMERICAN VALUES VIEWED THROUGH OTHER CULTURES

Vol. X The Elements of International Strategy: A Primer for the Nuclear Age
By Louis J. Halle

Vol. XI Nationalism and Internationalism: European and American Perspectives
By Erich Hula

Vol. XII Diplomacy and Values: The Life and Works of Stephen Kertesz in Europe and America
Edited by Kenneth W. Thompson

Vol. XIII Islamic Values and World View: Khomeyni on Man, the State and International Politics
By Farhang Rajaee

Vol. XIV Culture & Democracy: Anthropological Reflections on Modern India
By R. S. Khare

Vol. XV An Ambassador's Journey: An Exploration of People and Culture
By Charles Baldwin

Vol. XVI Selections From *The New American Commonwealth*
By Louis Heren

TABLE OF CONTENTS

Preface, Kenneth W. Thompson ix

Introduction xi

Chapter 1 A Comparative Sociology 1

Chapter 2 Culture and Democracy 13

Chapter 3 Social Dynamics of Indian Democracy 33

Chapter 4 Evaluation, Adequacy, and Ethos 49

Chapter 5 Concluding Remarks 79

References 85

PREFACE

Culture and Democracy is one of the final volumes in a Miller Center of Public Affairs series on American Values Projected Abroad. Appropriately, it throws the spotlight on India with whom the United States has much in common yet from whom it is separated by significant differences. Indo-American relations since India's independence some thirty-five years ago have been marked both by warmth and mutual trust and by political conflict and disputes. Some of the reasons are geo-political but others rest on the cultural differences so well-described in this study. The United States has sent some of its ablest political leaders and diplomats as ambassadors to India. It would be difficult to match the intellectual and moral qualities of men like Chester Bowles, John Sherman Cooper, John Kenneth Galbraith, Daniel Patrick Moynihan and Robert Goheen. In no Asian country has the pursuit of democracy been more highly valued. Indeed for Ambassador Bowles and others the prospects for democracy in the Third World were bound up with the future of India.

Others have been less positive about Indian politics and society. Tensions have developed and India and the United States have more than once found themselves on opposite sides of important questions in international politics. Indians have confronted Americans living in India with alleged affiliation with the CIA. Americans have condemned the Indians as arrogant and difficult to work with.

In part, the clevage between India and the United States may have roots in deepseated cultural differences. Professor R. S. Khare of the Department of Anthropology examines the sources of some of these differences. In India as in the United States, certain political goals and social arrangements are in tension if not open conflict with one another. For example, equality and hierarchy clash yet both are inherent in Indian culture today. Indian political leaders, particularly those that Professor Khare describes as transactional leaders, must balance and accommodate these conflicting goals. In this effort Khare has something in common with de Tocqueville's great effort to explain American democracy.

The Miller Center is fortunate that a world renowned anthropologist is one of its final contributors. Khare is not only a respected anthropologist but is founding chairman of the interdiscipling Committee on the Individual and Society. He has written on important topics in fields as diverse as cultural values and food and nutrition studies. He can only look forward to a distinguished career in the years ahead.

                                        Kenneth W. Thompson
                                        Director
                                        White Burkett Miller Center
                                            of Public Affairs
                                        University of Virginia

INTRODUCTION

This essay is the result of a slow but conscious and accumulating urge to view contemporary India in a comparative and comprehensive perspective. But this perspective, I thought, should neither be the captive of fully formal procedures of scholarship nor merely an ad hoc recapitulation of some popularly shared images and impressions. It should allow the ideas to range widely. Simultaneously, it was evident that though the social change studies of India in the last forty years or so were useful, they were neither sufficient nor always satisfactory for the purposes at hand. A new point of departure therefore seemed necessary, composed perhaps from across specialities. Culture and democracy, and India and America as two distinct societies, provided the thematic framework for such a departure. Though the risks were equally obvious: The path was untrodden and so little was systematically explored between Indian and American cultures, and culture and democracy, that only preliminary observations and analyses could be expected at this time. Yet such a beginning was appropriate.

To bring anthropology to study democracy as a part of Westernization, modernity, and diverse human condition is to seek new dialogues across social institutions, social forces, and cultural ideologies. It is also to admit a study of dilemmas, uncertainties, and ambiguities; they are seen as an essential part of the sociocultural reality, and of the general global condition. In democracy people "deconstruct" one certainty to strive toward another—a more democratic one. In Indian civilization, people have discovered uncertainty behind all kinds of certainties; they challenge certainty with uncertainties, and vice-versa. Indian democracy is also therefore found engaged in a similar exercise. It betrays some intrinsic cultural dispositions of the people. When events and relationships do not fall in a clear pattern, there may be cultural perplexities for anthropology to investigate but they may be neither useless nor meaningless. An anthropology of structures, controls, and certainties is incomplete unless joined by an anthropology of ambiguities, incomplete distinctions, and uncertainties. A study of total social reality demands both. This exercise on Indian culture and democracy attempts to illustrate the point.

Since such an attempt demands that one must stretch over the borders of one's speciality, an appropriate opportunity is usually necessary to trigger the inquiry. It came my way when Professor Kenneth W. Thompson, Director, White Burkett Miller Center of Public Affairs, University of Virginia, asked me if I could write for his Center an article on American values in relation to India. I accepted the offer essentially as a challenge to my almost exclusive focus on Indian studies. Subsequently, the article became the basis for the longer essay, again with the encouragement and understanding of Professor Thompson. As colleagues in different disciplines, we have shared a perceptive intellectual convergence over the years.

There is no better purpose to which this essay could be dedicated than to the hope of a genuine cultural understanding between India and America. They are not only two democracies but also two important cultures and peoples of the world who must contribute only their best to global human peace and harmony.

CHAPTER I

A COMPARATIVE SOCIOLOGY

An Unconventional Comparison and Context

When an anthropological comparison is proposed between the two complex cultures of India and America to study democracy, the topic quickly acquires a partly unconventional and partly problematic character. It is unconventional because one "normally" studies one or the other culture as a complete field of enquiry. To try to handle the two cultures together may be "too much," according to the prevalent wisdom of the specialist. The problem also becomes inordinately compounded if one chooses to compare the two cultures for such a complicated and value-loaded phenomenon as "democracy." Obviously the complications in studying democracy anthropologically are many, not the least of which is its vulnerability to partisanship and advocacy according to one's own political ideology and preference. More basically, therefore, we must ask: How is an anthropological study of democracy possible? And how far could a cultural comparison of India and America be useful in such a context? We will consider these questions in the opening section.

We will start with the assertion that the above issues are unavoidable for anthropology in today's world. It can neither dismiss nor dissolve them. Actually since anthropology may be increasingly inclined to analyse modern political and economic ideologies in comparative terms (e.g., Dumont 1977), such a subject as "culture and democracy" can no longer be regarded as beyond the scope of anthropological inquiry. This essay will therefore be an exercise in how might democracy as a cultural topic be pursued within anthropology and how a comparison of two distant and complex societies might provide a reliable context for the discussion of models, meanings, and dilemmas of contemporary democracy.

Though a sustained comparative analysis of the Indian and American cultures has yet to begin, several promising indicators already exist for such an attempt. In my view the outstanding general model of such a study is still Alexis de Tocqueville's *Democracy in America*. Though it compares two complex cultures of only the Western world in the middle of the nineteenth century, it provides an unique perspective on democracy as a comparative social experience. This study was remarkable as much for its insights and observations on democracy as a political value as for examining two complex (i.e. American and French) sociocultural systems. An anthropological study of democracy in the late twentieth century cannot but gain from such a research paradigm; and as an extension of Tocqueville's research plan, the next logical step consists in attempting a comparison of democracy across the Western and non-Western cultural divide.

However, such a project will be difficult as well as complicated for the reasons of what we already know or still do not know about democracy as a societal value and conduct. Though anthropological enquiry has gained a definite form and direction in the last half century, and though it has begun to take up the issue of politicoeconomic ideology in complex societies and nation-states, it is still most comfortable with small-scale political studies. It is still predominantly fascinated with specific cultural differences and contextual particulars. But, fortunately, of late microcosmic anthropological studies are also becoming a window to understand the larger comparative issues, especially as anthropological structuralism and symbology have gained as a method and perspective (e.g. Lévi-Strauss 1966; Dumont 1980; Schneider 1976; and Geertz 1973, 1983). However, since within this recent development there are still unworked issues and ambiguities, one can build only on some overlapping, congenial tendencies rather than discover a genuinely new direction.

Yet some recent studies have made highly relevant efforts and they produce a more congenial anthropological context for this attempt. For example, we may note three distinct types of attempts and their relevance to a comparative cultural study of India and America. First of all is the position that opposes ideologically India and the West, making a case for the total, irreconcilable differences between India and any Western culture, including American. Obviously, the cultural uniqueness of India is held supreme within this approach, while all relative symbolic and behavioral similarities are found spurious. Also, since India represents a civilizational complexity, the appropriate level of comparison should be with the West as a whole rather than with one of its specific cultures. This is the position of Louis Dumont, a French anthropologist, who shows one side of this argument by analysing the Indian hierarchical ideology (Dumont 1980), and the other side by examining the modern politicoeconomic ideology of the West (Dumont 1977, 1983)[1].

The second type of study attempts cultural synthesis. It is quite heterogeneous from within, ranging from topical journalistic observations to those provided by ambassadors (e.g. Bowles 1969) and earlier thinkers, philosophers and writers (e.g. Thoreau 1983; Emerson 1965; Whitman 1983; and James 1974). Though an interesting body of information to consider, our concern at present is only with those few that attempted a comparative anthropological or sociological synthesis.[2] For example, Milton Singer, a cultural anthropologist at the University of Chicago, offered us a comprehensive anthropological synthesis of an American (and European) understanding of India in a chapter called "Passage to More than India" (see Singer 1972: 11-38). This work is important for the issues expressed as well as implied. To an Indian living in America for about two decades, such writing provides a chance to probe into the American mind as it probes the Indian's.

Since Singer's type of anthropological writing is still rare, its value cannot be overemphasized for a meta-commentary like this one. Singer's attempt bases itself on some critical American cultural assumptions as it sketches "the 'natural' history of European and American images of India" (Singer 1972: 12). (Because of the limited scope of this essay, I shall have to exclude any direct discussion of European ideas about and images of India.) Essentially his assumptions are of two types, first those implicit in his general perspective and second those explicitly included and discussed in the essay. Singer recalls that interesting image of America of Walt Whitman where it is "the road between Europe and Asia," or of Thoreau where "Farthest India is nearer to me than Concord and Lexington" (quoted in Singer 1972: 22, 23). With such a subtle and profound intellectual empathy of the earlier American thinkers in the background, Singer shows not only how India has received a highly limited and variable attention in America over time, but also explains why this topic is worthy of a systematic and serious study, especially after a whole range of field studies conducted in India by American scholars since the Second World War.

I interpret Singer as proposing something for the other side as well: As Indian scholars come in greater contact with American culture and Americans, they should also study the two cultures comparatively from their background. However, the basic thrust of his analysis goes even deeper: Both American and Indian scholars should move beyond ad hoc observations and commentaries, and must get down to systematic, long-range research on the subject. This field of study should no longer depend only on stray perceptions and occasional political pronouncements by ambassadors or visiting political leaders. Instead, a two-way conceptual analysis is in order—of images, of formal and informal influences, and of varied similarities and differences. Simplified contrasts offered by "the spiritual East and the materialistic West" must not be allowed to abort the comparison even before it starts. Since much has been happening in this century and much more is now known, we should not only critique the simplistic assumption but be ready to discard it for a better one. Singer (1972: 36) finished his "passage to more than India" thus:

> Perhaps it [India] will now want to be a nation like other nations, rather than a topic of marvelous fables, or an object for self-righteous pity and charity, or the last home of occult mysteries. As India takes the path of modern nationalism, it will undoubtedly become less fascinating to the rest of the world, but it will also become less of an 'image' and more of a reality in that world.

The above observation tries to "concretize" India; it places India in the same twentieth century world in which all the West exists, with its hopes as well as fears. If it is the first necessary step to move beyond the stereotypes India has been a captive of[3], it is also to own all the problems of a modern state, of modernism, and of "progress." A study of modernity is as significant as its critique within the West. For it cannot be any other way toward the end of the century, when despite all the "progress," the future of all humanity faces a deepening uncertainty. It is as if new doubt, risk, and uncertainty are the ineluctable companions of "progress," and all nations, whether new or old or weak or strong, must contend with uncertainties from their own standpoints.

It is this aspect that Tocqueville could not have overlooked either, were he conducting his study of modern democracy in

A Comparative Sociology

America today. The enveloping ethos of new doubts, paradoxes, and uncertainties is something that large complex societies increasingly face in the last half of the twentieth century. Conversely, the quest of modern democracy for social certitude, economic equality, and individual freedom has run into unanticipated complications in this part of the century and a sociological attempt must study them as a central theme of inquiry to be responsive not only to the total social reality but to acquire a new perspective on democratic values as well. Modernity and democracy must be analyzed here as critically as tradition, and also both together as different forms of cultural information and communication rather than as two simple, evolutionary compartments, with "backwardness" standing for tradition and "progress" for modernity and modernization. To do so will be to learn from the "social change" studies of the fifties and the sixties in anthropology, and to gain from a critical analysis of democracy in the West (e.g. see Macpherson 1972, 1977). It will also be to place democracy in the wider context of the society in question, a step natural to an anthropological attempt and necessary to a comparative political analysis[4].

The two contexts of comparison, especially as represented by India and America, are marked by striking similarities and differences. Their historical and social distance remains essentially undiminished even if the recent political history and social expectations have produced an occasional convergence. To those, however, who see much more hope in this reverberation than only another confirmation of the East-West abyss, there is more to investigate, though cautiously and with appropriate analytic provisions. Most important, a comparative symbolic analysis is both feasible and appropriate. This approach is not simply about a comparison of particular cultural histories; it is at once deeper and wider, concerned with shared structures of ideas and tendencies among historically different sociocultural systems. Within this approach the specific hides the general, the unique the commonplace, and the substantive the symbolic. Historically distant though they are, the Indian and American cultures may now often speak to each other with the aid of cultural symbols, economic analogies, political homologies, and social vicissitudes. Though still seldom explored in this manner (but for a perceptive and pathbreaking exception, see Singer 1984), it is to this symbolic commerce that we should give more attention. To ignore it is to overlook an important exercise in cultural comparison.

Culture and Democracy

Approach, Context, and Focus

However, if such an attempt could still be found ad hoc and expedient by some, it would be not for the lack of an appropriate frame of inquiry. Nor will it be because the issues at stake are either superficial or inconsequential. For we must remember that a comparison between India and America takes up many vital ideas, conditions, and issues that speak to much wider issues. In a world where widest social, historical, and ideological differences must be increasingly faced in the garb of national policies and political interests (keeping international survival at stake), such a comparison is as inevitable as an attempt to *understand* the distant and the different by appropriate symbolic mechanisms. This is perhaps the way to learn about and communicate to the increasingly diverse nations towards the end of the century; the earlier nineteenth century approach that called to limit one's sharing with only those who had a shared ideology and history may be not only obsolete but dangerous. In such a perspective, India and America symbolize issues much more critical than the specific history and cultural pride of either. Actually, much significance lies in how each symbolizes tolerance to the other, and what both communicate about the larger human conditions and purposes, especially as they may share the concerns for democracy, world peace, and collective human survival.

However, a comparative symbolic analysis does not limit itself to a narrow range of relationships and conditions. It is not just an inquiry into the past or the present, the ideal or the practical, the inner or the outer, the abstract or the concrete, or the similar or the different. It moves through all such distinctions to get a perspective on the topic of study. Such a perspective may not be final but it tries to improve our explanation and understanding. The perspective forms as new relationships are recognized, old assumptions are revised and simplified, and logical contrasts are opened to account for ambiguity, irony, and paradox. Reality, even essential reality, is found distributed all over in such a perspective; hence there is a reluctance to define "total reality" either narrowly or once and for all. One also cannot circumscribe reality arbitrarily. There is intellectual openness in the approach but no tentativeness.

Considered within the above approach, India and America at present provide a repeated basis for shared modern cultural ideas, images, and experiences. We hold that such perspectives need to be characterized, compared, and commented upon. This is essentially what this study will try to do. No systematic exposition of a specific idea or condition can be expected at this stage of the inquiry. In this study "democracy" will mean a consideration of (a) diverse social experiences and relationships; (b) appropriate clusters of symbolic ideas, images, and categories; and (c) dilemmas, doubts, and differences at both conceptual and practical levels. All the three criteria will appear according to the context of discussion, rather than in a particular sequence. But to specify such an expanded domain of connotation for democracy is to convey the necessity of such a step for the proposed anthropological attempt. An unorthodox subject for anthropological analysis, democracy requires such a cultural contextualization. Anthropology approaches democracy in terms of people's ideas, symbols, and experiences; it also allows us to try to treat democracy as a part of the larger social contingency rather than only as a given political ideology and preference.

A comparison of India and America in the above context is diffused, difficult and complicated. There are hardly any systematic sociological studies to depend on, and hardly any perspectives to analyse or build upon. In such a situation what a characterizing study like this one can hope to accomplish will have to be illustrative and limited, rather than demonstrative and exhaustive. We will focus primarily on the Indian values, experiences, and contexts of democracy in the manner already specified. And there is a good reason for doing so: Democracy in India faces as well as raises serious questions of *justification and adequacy*. Though democracy is not an internal growth, as it is in the West, modern India has had clearly sympathetic tendencies. What causes this is perhaps the internal cultural heterogeneity itself. All kinds of symbols and symbolic relationships—analogies, homologies, reversals, etc.—help bring about such sympathies. Yet India remains a society "in which there is no total acceptance of any single end." It remains genuinely pluralist in means as well as ends. Unlike the West, it is undergoing several simultaneous political revolutions while in search of a commensurate political philosophy of its own.[5]

This essay will concern itself with selected sociocultural aspects and contexts of democracy between India and America. We will approach democracy as a part of the social experience of the people, and as representing a distinct model of man in moral, political, and economic terms. We will presume that, despite the Western political theory and philosophy it entailed in its formulation as a form of government, democracy gets strongly shaped by the cultural ideas and social conditions of a people. Hence India and America should be expected to exert their influence on democracy in their own ways, and both should be significant to study, singly as well as together. However, since the field of such a study is vast, we will confine ourselves severely to certain illustrative issues of the contemporary social complexity, making no attempt to link the discussion either to the Indian classical concepts of kingship, authority, power, and political state (for getting a sense of the field, see Dumont 1980; Altekar 1958; Coomaraswamy 1942), or to the issues in sociopolitical history of representative government in ancient and medieval India. This essay rests on the premise that democracy is most of all about a distinct model and meaning of man, and that India and America in the late twentieth century represent two major exercises directed toward a similar model of man, but borne by radically different historical and socioeconomic contexts. Wide differences, dilemmas, doubts, ambiguities, and uncertainties are a part of the two exercises, and they add to, rather than subtract from, the significance of the study.

Our contexts and contents of comparison between India and America will also be severely limited, oriented mostly to serve the above cultural view of democracy. For example, America will be approached as representing most of all a distinct democratic model of man, and a commensurate cluster of fundamental cultural values and viewpoints. America also represents to India a form of modernity. We will juxtapose these representations to the Indian ideas and experiences and make comparative observations. To do so will be both necessary and sufficient for the purposes of this essay, for, as already remarked, our goal is illustrative rather than exhaustive. Hence, for present purposes, at the heart of the comparison of India and America are the two models of democratic man, one recent, struggling and incomplete and the other embedded in a distinct way of life and values, and now increasingly identified as a distinct politicoeconomic ideology. Add to these two models of man the critical internal conflicts that India as a predominant culture and civilization brings and the scope of our comparison will be complete.

The contrasts between India and America as sociocultural systems readily stand out; they make the comparison of democracy more, not less, significant. But for such a comparison to flourish, we must at the outset grant that America represents a distinct but not unique sociocultural system; that America is not only a dominant politicoeconomic power structure but also a society with

A Comparative Sociology

shared human values, dilemmas and aspirations. Contrasts between India and America become more significant in such a perspective; they begin to communicate with each other for various reasons. America's sociocultural system is distinct since it has tried to shape itself in response to the demands of a representative democracy. Hence, if the democratic ideology of equality, liberty, and individualism has guided the American society, India, until recently, played out in its society the consequences of moral inequality, cultural tolerance, and spiritual liberation.

While the American culture developed in the last two centuries to imbibe, to substantiate, and to take the lead in the Western nations of liberal democracy and technological modernity, India exposed itself roughly in the same period to the Western colonial rule and to selected aspects of democracy. Only in the later half of this century did India become a democratic state by conscious political choice. But the significance of this exercise should not be incorrectly estimated. If it means renegotiating relationships between morality, power, wealth, and knowledge—all at once—by an entire civilization, it also means a spate of new value conflicts and major social realignments, tensions, distortions, and disappointments. In such a society, the past does not yield the expected certainty, only a similitude; the present promises but does not deliver; and the future remains unpredictable.

Yet India must learn to reckon with changing times, even as it puts Western democracy to new tests by its own non-Western values and fractious social experience. For, actually, India tests Western democracy as much as democracy tests India; any success or failure must equally reflect on both. (The earlier leader-follower model is biased and incomplete; hence untenable.) Outside the Western world, India's tests with democracy are significant for their size and complexity, but, more importantly, they provide a critical non-Western commentary on the justification, functioning, adequacy, and sufficiency of democracy. As democracy tests the Indian models of man with its own, and as the Indian models test the democratic model, a lot of cultural representation, interpretation, and characterization goes on, as we shall see.

There is a wider significance of such an evaluation of democracy towards the end of the twentieth century. Democracy, despite all of its ideological significance in geopolitics, remains a fragile notion in everyday life; it is insecure, uncertain, and only incompletely known to major populations of the world. Political theorists, philosophers, and social theorists have already raised questions about the future of liberal democracy (e.g. see Macpherson 1972, 1977; Berlin 1978, Chapter 7; and Dahrendorf 1979, Chapter 5 and 6). A cultural account of democracy is now critical because any viable political theory, which claims to be universal, cannot discount the distinct role of diverse cultural values in democracy. It is especially true when the non-Western world is concerned, and when democracy aspires to provide a human model of "self-government" for the world at large.

Democracy in a country like India requires perhaps both—an anthropological study of democracy and a political theory that will test the West generated models and criteria of democracy and will develop those true to the Indian ideas and experience. Anthropological insights must constantly guide and renew the political theory, since only the two together can help answer the larger issues of status, power, and self-government within a state. If a political theory posits and explains the core values of democracy over time, anthropology evaluates it against the actual diversity of cultural values and social experience.[6]

Notes

1. Louis Dumont is also significant to us for invoking Tocqueville to set up the value contrast. If Dumont utilizes Tocqueville to represent the Western ideology to the Indian (where his most likely representative will be Manu), I approach Tocqueville for inherent and unavoidable value comparisons. For me contrasts do not tell the entire story, however well abstracted and however uniquely juxtaposed. Human cultural systems, both in idea and behavior, are fundamentally the arrangements of meaningful—relatively meaningful—communications; the people of a culture make sure that such communications continue to be socially shared to make sense of themselves as well as the other. In the way Tocqueville is used here, his analysis shows how the West betrays differences as well as similarities in relation to the late twentieth century India. Logically as well as culturally, contrast is only one dimension of the mental procedure called "comparison." It does not, and cannot, stand for the whole procedure even if a method of study rests itself on ideological abstractions and their uniqueness.
2. It seems that no major Indian sociologist or anthropologist has undertaken a sustained comparative study of the Indian and American cultures. The point is significant by itself and is worth remarking. For our present purposes, I shall observe that the post-forties popular Indian attitude towards America has been ambivalent. It is usually of fascination and imitation when the images of material prosperity,

science and technology, and freer social life-styles are concerned. Yet any close range view of American culture and its architecture remains mostly alien to the Indian, whether he is an intellectual or not. When it comes to enduring cultural ideas and philosophy, America only rarely draws attention of the Indian mind. At this level all that is enduring and substantive in America is subsumed within the Western, mainly European, thought. Whether the twentieth century achievements of America will significantly alter this general image, is still too early to know. However, for the last several decades the influence of American economics, science and culture has considerably increased. It is now a social fact worthy of study by itself.

3. Actually, in recent times the role of educated Indians is not insignificant in perpetuating the spiritualist-materialist dichotomy and the image of the fabled, mysterious India within India and abroad. Partly under imitation, partly to depict India as distinct and unique, and partly to retain their own cultural naivete, educated Indians more often transmitted what they received about India from the Western counterpart rather than thought the issues through themselves. The Indian cultural past quickly became either a dead weight or an irretrievable but inseparable "golden age" replete with all the wonders that was India. The enlightened twentieth century intellect must therefore resist the temptation to equate simply the West with all the present and future, and India with only the past (e.g. see Nehru quoted in Singer 1972: 36-37). A society, even as a modern nation, must learn itself to live well with its past before it can explore the present and leap into the future. If anywhere, it has to be true for India; its living past requires a genuine and honest approach from the Indian himself. No quick denials or West-inspired modernist rejections may suffice to alter the reality, a point that Independent India's ethnic and communal cleavages amply corroborate.

4. A comparative political analysis at present needs to examine, rather than assume, the critical superiority and certainty of the Western political values. It is especially useful when India is being studied. India's society and history refuse any simplified, ad hoc, or a priori juxtaposition to the West. They both stand on their own on the one hand, yet they are not strangers to each other on the other. Their ambivalence runs deep; it is immediate as well as long-standing.

5. We can reliably refer to Isaiah Berlin on the point (1978: 143-172). Judging by his criteria, India will be a suitable place to look for the development of a political philosophy: "It follows the only society in which political philosophy in its traditional sense, that is, an inquiry concerned not solely with elucidation of concepts, but with the critical examination of presuppositions and assumptions, and the questioning of the order of priorities and ultimate ends, is possible, is a society in which there is no total acceptance of any single end." However, post-Gandhi India is submerged in intense everyday politics. Politi-

cians rather than political philosophers and theorists are the men of the moment. But this may scarcely mean the end of a need for adequate political philosophy in India, perhaps only a preparation towards it. Not unlike the West, where so many competing orders of political priorities and values are emerging, and where whatever was culturally certain is politically doubted and disputed now, India is also entering a period of self-doubts. Indian value concepts and their validity face conflicting social criteria, drifting in new and unpredictable directions.

6. There is also a subtler influence to be recognized: Democratic values may have influenced anthropology as well as political theory in the West, especially in the second half of this century. Anthropology's liberalism, humanism and relativism, whether historical or ethical or epistemological, are not only influenced by the Western democratic values but are perhaps determined by some critical historical events (e.g. see Hatch 1983, for a discussion of the role of World War II on anthropological relativism). Indian anthropology and sociology essentially share the same ethos of liberal humanism and relativism, though the post-Independence experience has qualified it in various ways. In order to become critically significant, Indian anthropology and sociology may have to engage in a systematic self-analysis: How closely are India and Indian experience reflected in anthropology's liberalism and relativism? How universal is the West-produced universal, and how should one treat such limits for additional insights rather than more polemics? This is perhaps also the dilemma of the political theory which promises us to give a considered perspective on democracy.

Even in the West, anthropological humanism has yet to come to grips with such a late twentieth century development as the rise of fundamentalism in religion and politics. It has yet to move beyond the sixties (but see Dumont 1977: 9-28). Since anthropology must concern itself with non-Western societies all over the globe, whether nations (including where democracy can only be an incomplete and alien experience) or not, it must be prepared for rigorous self-examination; it must admit its own value preferences and limitations (cf. Dumont 1977: Chapter 1; Dumont 1980). That it cannot be above these is better to recognize openly rather than to claim somehow an impregnable moral neutrality. To do so might be helpful for another reason: Anthropology will be able to analyse and explain value charged human issues and conditions according to its roots in liberalism, humanism, and relativism. Whether immediately popular or not, such explanations and insights will remain true to the anthropological spirit of genuine global humanism. Though sensitive to regional and local human history, society, and culture, such an anthropology cannot be the captive of a region (even if that region is "Western"). It is the contention of this essay that only such an anthropology could be well suited to study democracy.

CHAPTER 2

CULTURE AND DEMOCRACY

We may return to Tocqueville's study, *Democracy in America,* to set the stage for our further discussion. His method is helpful to us, since his premises and propositions approach the issues of ideology, society and politics in terms of culturally significant criteria.[1] He did not set up outright compartments and oppositions between France and America in the middle of the last century; we do not need to do so between India and America at the end of the twentieth century. If his discussion remained sensitive to the complexity of transitions within the American society, which was then a relatively new nation, we must maintain a similar stance for India now. Neither a simple reductionist nor a panegyric, he held on fast to the main theme of his inquiry—American democracy and "progress of equality"; one similarly needs to be aware of the complexities and distractions as India is approached (e.g. see Tocqueville 1969: xi–xii; 9–20; 417–418). Such methodological precautions help interpret Tocqueville more widely than his specific concern with only Western Christian states and their democracies.

Tocqueville also showed how democracy should be considered a part of the larger society and its values. If democracy tends to influence life-styles, it has also to contend with opposing, heterogeneous forces, including those he called "aristocratic" (or hierarchical). He saw democracy producing new similarities and differences in America; it may be no different in India. If he showed that democracy influences the social values, philosophy, and world view of a people, he also pursued them in the context of the changes in law, politics, and economics. In other words, democracy cannot be studied only as a compartment of political theory or philosophy; once seriously taken up by a nation, it must contend with people's criteria of everyday life. (For some illustrative discussions, see

Tocqueville 1969 Vol. 2, Part I pp. 429-442; Part II pp. 503-513; Part III pp. 572-594). Recently, a political theorist quoted Dewey to underscore the wider—one may say anthropological—dimensions of democracy this way: "Democracy is a way of life"; it is concerned with "the art of full and moving communication"; it encourages production by a "method of cooperative intelligence" (Macpherson 1977: 73-75).[2]

As Tocqueville amply showed in his classical study, the interrelationships between democratic processes and a people's cultural background are deep, diverse, and even tumultuous at times. India, an old culture and a new democracy, and America, a preeminent democracy and a new culture, offer a complex and rich commentary on comparative interrelationships between culture and democracy. One of our complementing propositions will be that once a people take the democratic process seriously, it begins to enter and shape certain matters of personal identity and family life in a clear manner. Whether slow in coming or incomplete or culturally hybridized, such directions must become evident sooner or later in a new democracy.

Implicit Resemblance

India and America offer an interesting comparison in this regard; they are similar in some ways yet quite dissimilar in other ways. Consider the American society of 1848 about which Tocqueville wrote (when America was already a practicing democracy for about sixty years) and compare it with India today, a country independent for over thirty-five years, but there will still be a basis for discovering some genuine similarities and parallels. They will be there for two reasons, first because of the shared human needs, demands and satisfactions, and second because democracy generates similar social expectations wherever it goes. Yet while Indians may seek to establish new rules to guarantee equal opportunity, open access to education, freedom of speech, and inalienable civil equality, it may neither take the same path that the American experience took, nor may it succeed or fail in the same manner, and to the same extent. The criteria of performance, adequacy, and satisfaction will differ. It is only to be expected. Today's India therefore has to be a hotchpotch of indigenous forces and external influences; its society may undo a tradition here and violate a democratic value there, and yet it may neither disown the traditional nor the democratic forces. The Indian democratic process may thus be slow, tortuous, and ambiguous, but it is a genuine exercise, nevertheless.

Given the immensity of historical and cultural differences between America and India, the journey of democracy in the two countries cannot be expected to be smooth. Hasty comparisions and conclusions must therefore be avoided. Thus while Tocqueville could describe the completion of a democratic process in America with confidence, we as yet cannot do the same for India. India must go through much more social experience, internally as well as externally, to anchor and evolve its own version of democracy. In this process, India may make its own contribution to the theory and practice of democracy in the non-Western context. This means that while we may have to withhold our overall estimation of the Indian experience, it does not diminish the significance of a Tocqueville-style comparative study of the contemporary Indian culture and democracy. Most of Tocqueville's premises, propositions, and arguments remain open for a rigorous study under the Indian evidence. Even the refutations of Tocqueville will be significant under such a circumstance, but no summary rejection.

However, to draw upon Tocqueville's example is neither to minimize the complexity of the issue of culture and democracy in the twentieth century, nor to sweep aside the substantial differences and estrangements between India and America. Still, it means not to underestimate resemblances in ideas, symbols and experiences. It means to let the analogous values and experiences count for what they are, resisting the opposite mistake—to keep India and America incommunicado beyond the topical trivia afforded by the late twentieth century journalism and geopolitical considerations. It is to reject the formulation that India and America, as two geographically distant and economically unequal nations, can only represent unbridgeable divisions and oppositions and little else. The prospect for a better perspective on what India and American represent appears when the cultural values and practical forces are considered together as a part of the total social reality and are allowed to take us as far as they can. In this view each society has its own distinct cultural value of man; both are also practicing democracies, with a democratic model of man. However, we must resist the temptation to reduce the Indian and American models to a simple characterization. It will become clearer as we pursue our discussion. To India, America represents democracy and modernity; to America, India is a diverse traditional society with modern democracy. Hence each has its own ways of approaching democracy and of responding to its contextual political, legal, and economic forces.

Democracy itself may have several faces and versions when two countries like India and America are under consideration. Though both have at present a constitution-based, legally enforced democracy and both may depend variously on earlier models of the Western liberal democracy, India, as a non-Western developing country, must differ from America in its approach and response to democracy (see Macpherson 1972). If America has developed its culture for the last two centuries essentially in relation to democracy, to India modern democracy came from the West, mostly in this century via uneven, conflict-ridden developments from both within and without (e.g. the British). Yet such a difference remains culturally flat, largely uniformative beyond a point. More accurately, while India and America have subjected modern democracy to their own values and life experiences, shaping democracy as it has shaped them, India must reckon with its long, diverse and tumultuous social past. As it does so, India confronts modern democracy with its own values of legitimate authority, representational power, and social justice. India's social diversity makes modern democracy a many-faceted, even disjointed affair for the most.

Not only are there several popular versions of modern democracy in India but also shifting models of what is a "good rule" and "a good ruler." There are long-standing cultural views on the ideal polity (e.g. as in Rāmarājya) and rigorous expectations from a government (a *sarkār*). Modern democracy is also only a form of government to most Indians; it is there to deliver, to protect, and to be just (not only as the government sees fit but as the people expect it to be). The government must be dependable, and must always be there to fall back upon. In contrast America disparages pervasive government; it should let people govern themselves "with a light touch." Both India and America are participatory democracies and both work with their own criteria for "vote banks" to elect political representatives, but both differ in their attitudes towards those in power and authority.

India approaches authorities and leaders under the guru-father paradigm of social acceptance (often called *māi-bāpa* by those inferior and dispossessed); America views them as representative-performers to uphold a public trust (see Tocqueville 1969:95). Even for modern India, to recall two Weberian categories, leaders are always a *mixture* of traditional and rational authority; where one ends and the other begins is often blurred in everyday life.

Such personal values as "courage, endurance, fearlessness, and above all self-sacrifice" form the core of an ideal leader in India, according to Gandhi (e.g. see Gandhi quoted in Bondurant 1965:171). He saw leaders guided by duties rather than by offices, personal rights, and substantial perquisites. However, again, everyday life in India turns back on this rather lofty ideal, where "transactional leadership," to use a distinction of James MacGregor Burns (1978), dominates that "transformational." America does not differ that much in this regard. As Burns amply shows, transactional leadership, where political favors must be exchanged, is entrenched in America, though, not unlike India, it also appreciates and longs for the transformative leadership that concerns the realization of "higher goals"—justice, equality, liberty. Yet India and America follow their own styles of "transactional" leadership, and each learns to tolerate the transgressions of its own politicians by social context and prevalent values of patronage. Comparatively, India is in much greater social flux; here politics has become a way of seeking routine goods and services, and the politician a pervasive, all-purpose power broker.

Hierarchy and Democracy: Clash and Coexistence

If democracy represents modernity to India, hierarchy is a basic and pervasive fact of traditional life. That it is a fundamental aspect of Indian society and civilization has already been shown (see Dumont 1980). Since India is long used to postulating and channeling social inequalities via caste orders, democracy must contend with an entrenched and intricate system already in place. No wonder therefore that caste and democracy have become grist for political analysis for the last half of this century. What most often interests the specialists is the "complexity" of this encounter. For what is complex is also intricate, intense, variable, and unpredictable—all at once. Empirical studies of localities, elections, political conflicts, and party realignments continue rather unabated (for a general review, see Morris-Jones 1971; specific studies include, Brass 1965; Weiner 1967, 1968; Morris-Jones 1971; Kothari 1970; Weiner and Kothari 1965). This growing knowledge cautions us against oversimplification.

Neither democracy nor hierarchy is a simple, static pole of opposition in India. Even as we recognize that democracy's essence is equality, and hierarchy rests on inequality, both release diverse social forces. Each at present stakes out its claims in India, with or without direct conflict, and each learns to modify the other as a part of the larger exercise in clash and coexistence. But since the clash is not superficial, and since it is of civilizational ideals and values (as shown clearly by Dumont 1977, 1980), the Indian exercise points toward two more fundamental points: first, human cultures, however completely antipodal, always remain capable of forging new communications across the divide; second, such communications tend to be tumultuous, conflict-ridden and prolonged. No easy, quick resolutions may work; the reality may bring about the unexpected, but there is no reason to doubt the seriousness of such an exercise. To remark this way is only to recall the Western experience of democracy and class. As Macpherson (1977) shows, democracy in the West has oscillated several times between the utopian and liberal formulations, and there is no resolution in sight.

If anything, India's case must remain more complex, especially since, unlike the West, hierarchy plays culturally different games with notions of "class," "property," "land," "ownership," and "production." Historically, these games have also changed; sometimes even the rules of the game have been challenged. The last half of the twentieth century has done so again, and this time via the Indian adoption of liberal democracy. What the West has already experienced, India is also discovering: A "fit" between democracy and social inequality is more difficult in practice than political theories and models propose. The best a country can do is to make several approximations to reduce or diffuse political and economic antagonisms at the same time as the people's rights and participation are increased. But as Macpherson (1977:10) points out, a vicious circle awaits such a society:

> The reduction of social and economic inequality is unlikely without strong, democratic action. And it would seem, whether we follow Mill or Marx, that only through actual involvement in joint political action can people transcend their consciousness of themselves as consumers and appropriators. Hence the vicious circle: we cannot achieve more democratic participation without a prior change in social inequality and in consciousness, but we cannot achieve the changes in social inequality and consciousness without a prior increase in democratic participation.

India is experiencing the workings of this vicious circle in its own way as hierarchy and democracy confront each other not only as models but as forces of everyday life. And what the opposed logic of the two models cannot negotiate, people's daily activities do because they must, to remain practicable yet meaningful. Democracy and hierarchy compromise in India in a distinct way: Caste generates the sociopolitical motive and organization for throwing up formal "democratic leadership." Sociologically an "odd couple," each learns to work its way through the other, even if it also means that each must modify some of its essence in the process. In turn, democracy gives caste such "modern causes" to pursue as equal citizenship and national "welfare," even if such causes will be paradoxical.

The American system, as Lloyd Warner had noted (1962:126-152), also proceeds with the help of the same two antithetical social principles—equality and status—which mark the Indian scene, though with reversed social primacy:

> It is clear to those of us who have made studies in many parts of the United States that the primary and most important fact about the American social system is that it is composed of two basic, but antithetical, principles: the first, the principle of equality; the second, the principle of unequal status and of inferior and superior rank. The first declares that all men are equal and that all men must have equal opportunity to get the good things of life. The second, seldom openly stated but nevertheless potent and powerful, makes it evident that Americans are not always regarded as equal and that many of the values they treasure, that provide them with a will to do and to achieve, can continue to exist only as long as they have a status system. I wish to affirm that, paradoxical as it may seem, both these antithetical principles, when properly balanced, are necessary for the proper functioning of contemporary American democracy. (Warner 1962: 127-128.)

In India everybody is born with a social status and then tries to make his career under the democratic rules of the Indian state. If the status continues to matter a lot, it now has to contend with the democratic emphasis on equal opportunity for all. Recalling Tocqueville, if America was born with a passion for equality, India has long been a land of social hierarchy. Issues of contract and status, and rights and duties face each other directly, especially within urban families.

Actually we could characterise this condition with a quotation from Tocqueville on what happens when the bonds of social hierarchy begin to loosen up, willy-nilly, and when the established values of moral authority and obligations blur and weaken within the family and outside.

> As the rules of social hierarchy are less strictly observed, as great ones fall and the humble rise, as poverty as well as wealth ceases to be hereditary, the distance separating the master and woman daily diminishes both in fact and in men's minds (Tocqueville 1969: 528).

The urban families in India now show the influence of such forces, allowing the younger generation to speak out on career and marriage. Once employed and married, social independence of the urban youth increases. They usually follow modern occupations, going wherever opportunities are available and wherever a future placement will take them. This social tendency is usually found to have multiple consequences when juxtaposed to the traditional hierarchical scheme. The family dislocates itself from the traditional criteria of local status; its economic survival and social position link directly to the modern careers of its members (particularly its head); the criteria of caste and kinship status get suitably modified by civil contracts; the role of the ancestral past diminishes, and "the woof of time is ever being broken" (Tocqueville 1969: 507). The hereditary basis for prosperity begins to slacken under such circumstances in urban India. The "family interest" becomes distinct and often uppermost. Families coordinate and express caste interests (with "self-interest" variously expressed through families). (Compare Tocqueville's [1969: 507-508] characterization where families continually rise and fall under democracy.) The democratic forces are thus found punctuating, bending, and sometimes severing the larger traditional links of the Indian family. The traditional ancestral history and its criteria become distant while the present struggles for family fortune engage one the most. Since the urban individual achiever is still firmly embedded in his extended family, his family moves up whenever his career moves up (or vice-versa). He is still, however, far away from the individual isolation Tocqueville assigns to a completed democratic revolution. Actually, the Indian may not duplicate the American experience.

Major realignments are occurring in urban India as the democratic rules are taking hold for distributing the expanding economic goods and services, as the caste occupations lose their social glamour and economic value, and as the forces of government, law, market, and politics shape the Indian. The traditional privileges of the higher caste are challenged while those of the middle and lower castes try to move up on the economic, political, and social scales. Thus, the social realignments occurring in India may be generally analogous to the condition described by Tocqueville (1969: 508-509; my interpolations):

> Those who once held the highest ranks [e.g. the Brahmans] in the subverted hierarchy cannot forget their ancient greatness at once ... They regard all those whom society now makes their equals as oppressors whose fate could not concern them; they have lost sight of their former equals and no longer feel tied by common interests to their lot.... But those formerly at the bottom of the social scale [e.g. the Untouchables] and now brought up to the common level by a sudden revolution cannot enjoy their new-found independence without some secret uneasiness: there is a look of fear mixed with triumph in their eyes.

As Tocqueville repeatedly pointed out in his analysis, democracy must distinctly realign individuals to different groups, and varied groups reorient among themselves. The same is now pervasively occurring in India; castes, regional linguistic groups, sects, and communal groups—all realign themselves to retain or enhance their economic and political resources. They try to survive the new world of competition and contracts. The contestants strive for tolerable parity and fairness on the immediate basis and expect full equality in an ultimate sense. The social battles for fairness, justice, and equality become sharper in proportion to the popular acceptance of democratic expectations. Yet in a country like India social divisions, regional differences, and ethnic loyalties remain deep and constantly fuel social discords with those who claim equality. The democratic expectations also render the traditional norms of inequality unbearable in new ways. Though status is important to him, and he behaves and speaks hierarchically all the time, the Indian also engages in a democratic rhetoric to challenge the norms of both hierarchy and inequality. This social exercise is largely symptomatic and uneven but pervasive and significant nevertheless; its character, as is to be expected, is strikingly Indian but its completion beyond the horizon.

The realignment of social groups in democratic India also includes the creation of increasingly more voluntary associations (cf. Hsu 1963). Most often assembled for non-traditional social purposes, a voluntary group incorporates egalitarian principles for its formal agenda. People protest when these are violated in practice. With mushrooming unions of the widest variety of workers in India, most of the associations variously approach the serious goals of economic and political fairness. They function to help distribute fair wages according to the importance of a group's work, keeping up with changing economic and political conditions. Thus, though assembled and run by the same Indians who belong to traditional families and ranked caste groups, they play the game differently outside. They realize that the egalitarian, democratic rules of a formal organization are designed to contest and influence the government policies and programs towards the workers. The rise and adaptation of such groups in India is indicative of the sociological fact that the caste ethic, though still entrenched in certain sectors, does not preclude the formation and functioning of alternative groups with alternative ideas and ethics.

The cultural significance of the issues involved in hierarchy and democracy cannot be underestimated in India. Their conflicts are as important as their practical compromises. This is because Indian hierarchy treats some forms of social inequalities as a part of the larger cultural values and world views. Social separations and distances are awarded unique cultural meanings, as Dumont (1980 [1970]) showed, and democracy has to make sense in this background. The Indian social hierarchy is therefore not the same as Western class rankings, and the interrelationships between Western democracy and class are only a useful approximation but no substitute for a systematic empirical and conceptual study of the Indian social experience. With this caveat in place, what follows helps raise a preliminary anthropological discussion on an important subject.

Indian Ideas of Democracy

India approaches democracy with its uniquely intricate schemes of social precedence; it invokes its own ideas and experiences about equality and political representation. Again, while systematic studies are required of how and why the nineteenth and early twentieth century Indian leaders and reformers justified democracy to India, wide-ranging general indicators are already available (for example, for an influential train of ideas in contemporary India, see Gandhi 1959 [1947]: 15-21; Tagore 1971 [1922], 91-140;

and Nehru 1981 [1946]; for a brief but very useful discussion, see Joshi 1979: 33-50). Roughly, since India's quest for political freedom meant liberty and representation for all, democracy appealed naturally, though neither without reservations about the Western liberal model nor without tredipations about its popular use in India. Gandhi accepted democracy as a part of his definition of *swarāj* ("self-rule") and as a route to "true" individual freedom — that is the one achieved "under a regime of Unadulterated *Ahimsā*" (non-violence). Despite his full awareness of caste ideology and practice, he made "true democracy" his religious and political creed. Democracy was launched in India with such personal convictions. If Gandhi sought it as a configuration of politico-religious values indispensable to him (e.g. by trust, nonviolence, duty, and fearlessness), Nehru gave the Indian democracy its institutions after the Independence. Each provided a corrective to the other (Joshi 1979: 38).

Still, Gandhi had a greater grasp of the indigenous cultural concepts, categories and values, whether they conflicted with democratic ideas or not. His ideas came nearer to the people's, and spoke to the institutions of inequality and injustice. This is anthropologically significant, though we should expect to find there valuable glimpses rather than scholarly tracts. Reading him helps discover how he tried to translate the best in the Western democratic tradition to relate it to the values and contexts internal to India. Although he could be easily faulted for an incomplete and even ambiguous translation, he was an earnest translator, ready to test the impact of his translation on other Indian leaders and the masses.[3] Democracy meant for him the widest participation and representation, up to each village and every individual, and irrespective of whether one was weak or strong (see Gandhi 1959: 15-19, and related segments). Most importantly, democracy was never only a theory or a doctrine for him; it was seen as the part of a comprehensive, moral life-style.[4] But its vulnerbility was as obvious to him as its strengths:

> The greater the institution the greater [are] the chances of abuse. Democracy is a great institution and therefore it is liable to be greatly abused. The remedy therefore is not avoidance of democracy but reduction of possibility of abuse to a minimum. (Gandhi 1959: 15).

How does Gandhi approach the two critical issues for Indian democracy — socioreligious heterogeneity and caste inequality?

Though he may have underestimated the actual strength of both, his unyielding faith in human goodness allowed him to see beyond them. By doing so he also set a difficult moral goal before the Indian democracy: "*Pūrna swarāja* (Complete self-rule)," Gandhi's democracy, "is as much for the prince as for the peasant, as much for the rich landowner as for the landless tiller of the soil, as much for the Hindus as for the Mussalmans, as much for Parsis and Christians as for the Jains, Jews, and Sikhs, irrespective of any distinction of caste or creed or status in life." Such a formulation reflects the Indianization of democracy in all critical essentials.

Emulating the Gandhian model in all political essentials, Nehru, the other major architect of Indian democracy, pursued as well as modified the Indianization of Western democracy. As he gave shape to the actual functioning of democratic institutions in independent India, he saw the limits of both dream and reality. Eclectic in political philosophy, he would seek the best of two different systems for India—democracy and socialism. He saw limitations in both, independently as well as in relation to the Indian circumstance. Yet India, according to him, needed the best of both (see Brecher 1959: 527), "in which both sectors (public and private) of the economy could cooperate to mutual advantage." Mookerjee (1972: 20) quotes André Malaraux (in his *Antimemoires*) to impress the cardinal point that if Nehru was devoted to the cause of social justice, his commitment to "just means" was equally strong: "To imagine that an army of ten million communists were cheerfully transforming the kingdom of Prince Siddharta into popular communes as in China." Nehru had himself commented on this issue and on the role of India's past in its present and future by invoking Gandhi:

> It has always seemed to me remarkable how he [Gandhi] could link the past with the present and even the future ... The most vital lesson that he taught us or make us remember afresh, was the importance of means. Ends were never enough by themselves, for the ends were shaped by the means that lead to them. If there is any basic truth in the principle and in this method of working, then we also have to build on the foundations he laid down. (Nehru et. al. 1962: 9-10).

Democracy provided for both change and continuity, according to Nehru, though one could not be oblivious to the entrenched vested interests against change (Nehru et. al. 1962: 19). Yet he found change inevitable for the twentieth century India; science, technology, humane values, and self-pride—all should contribute. And not unlike Gandhi, he was not to be satisfied with "material progress" alone; he was concerned about "the quality and depth of our people." For in the same Azad Memorial Lecture delivered in 1959, Nehru had remarked (1962: 4):

> I have often wondered that if our race forgot the Buddha, the Upanishads, and the great epics, what then will it be like? It would be uprooted and would lose the basic characteristics which have clung to it and given it distinction throughout these long ages. India would cease to be India.

The above discussion justifies a cultural view of Indian democracy, especially via Gandhi and Nehru.[5] In it are also embedded, one could argue, a number of issues of anthropological concern. Nehru is, for example, found to be remarkably sensitive to interrelationships between history and culture, and to the complexity of processes of social change in India. All of this was evident even before the social scientists had conducted their studies in India in the fifties and the sixties (e.g. see Nehru 1981 [1946]). More than Gandhi, his views on caste in modern India were unambiguous: " ... I want the narrow conflicts of today in the name of religion or caste, language or province, to cease, and a classless and casteless society to be built up where every individual has full opportunity to grow according to his worth and ability. In particular, I hope that the curse of caste will be ended, for there cannot be either democracy or socialism on the basis of caste." (Nehru 1962: 43-44). But at the same time, noncoercive means were integral to his view of democracy:

> It is sometimes said that rapid progress cannot take place by peaceful and democratic methods and that authoritarian and coercive methods have to be adopted. I do not accept this proposition. Indeed, in India today any attempt to discard democratic methods would lead to disruption and would thus put an end to any immediate prospect of progress. From the long term point of view also I believe in the dignity of the individual and in as large a measure of freedom for him as possible, though in a complex society freedom has to be limited lest it injure others. (Nehru 1962: 39).

Culture and Democracy

This quotation not only gives us a glimpse of one of his fundamental convictions but also reflects perhaps the irreplaceable *terra firma* that the Western democracy had for him. Hence, what he was found saying on October 13, 1949, before both houses of the U.S. Congress, was not superficial. After quoting the preamble of the Indian constitution, he had remarked:

> You will recognize in these words that I have quoted an echo of the great voices of the founders of your republic. You will see that though India may speak to you with a voice that you may not immediately recognize or that may perhaps appear somewhat alien to you, yet in the voice there is strong resemblance to what you have often heard before. (Nehru 1950: 6).

The two founders of modern democracy in India, Gandhi and Nehru, recognized democracy not only as a justified form of government but also as an uncompromising social value for a whole new nation. If democracy started as a political strategy of the colonized for seeking freedom, it became a moral conviction and nationally accepted just procedure with Gandhi and the Indian National Congress. Hence justification of democracy in India essentially preceded rather than followed political independence, and it was at once moral and political at the hands of Gandhi. Positive experience of the freedom movement verified its value for the national leaders as well as the common man. The Indian masses came to know how to become participants in a political cause and local politicians discovered a way to become democratic representatives. This dimension of Indian democracy is significant to remember to realize that its experience, explanation and justification have followed a cultural and historical course started about one hundred years ago. The issues of social clash and coexistence have also been unfolding ever since for the Indian democracy. Though caste and democracy have been strange bedfellows in India, with ever increasing quarrels, each still modifies rather than annihilates the other, with tolerance a longtime characteristic of India. Whether it can remain so is something only the future will tell, but meanwhile no simple theories of ideological opposition and conflict can explain the Indian condition better. A healthy skepticism is always in order but not simple exclusions based on one's enthnocentrism.[6]

Differences and Difficulties Persist

A central issue that this essay must stress is before us. The issues hidden behind hierarchy and democracy in India, we will show, are rich and diverse; they are much more various than a total logical and cultural opposition can convey, though the differences with the Western democratic idea and experience are neither limited nor superficial. The differences are diverse, even disparate, but not divergent. The Indo-European cultural dynamics, old and new, is responsible, at the most fundamental level, one may assert, for setting such limits. There will be little gained by comparison if India and the West were only representing an infinite sequence of differences between the two and the two were implied to move away relentlessly from each other, with unlikelihood of any overlap (resemblance) and concordance (communication). Human cultures differ, diversify, and even diffuse but seldom as rigorously and completely as the logic of total opposition would propose or imply. Such an obvious point is worth mentioning only because it will allow us to restore a panoply of relations and contents to a cultural comparison between India and America.

While such a step is methodologically critical to make a comparative study of India and the West possible, a rigorous examination of India and America still remains difficult. There are several reasons. First, differences between them could be anywhere from a contrast and contradiction to a simple variation. (Economic and military contrast usually aborts a study before it starts.) Second, overlaps between the two cultures could be symbolic and conceptual, and could be hidden behind a surface contrast. (Conversely, a surface resemblance may gloss over a deeper gap.) Third, their similarities and differences, whether superficial or deep, may be scattered in widely different fields—from philosophical to economic, to scientific and technological—to thwart any quick and simple study of cultural assumptions. Fourth, both cultures may retain certain convergent ideas, concepts, categories, either implicit or incompletely formulated. Both may award provisional significance to each other's major cultural contributions (e.g. Indian notion of nonviolence and American technological ingenuity). Fifth, one or several prevalent cultural biases and images (e.g. for tradition or fads) may distract the investigator from reaching contemporary values more basic or fundamental to both.

A comparison between Indian and American democracy is beset with all such difficulties. But since the difficulties are a part of the

Culture and Democracy

cultural communication between them and are also a commentary on the modern intellectual temper, they provide an added justification for such a comparison. Further, since India's hierarchy and democracy illustrate differences internally (i.e. within India as a cultural system and country) as well as externally (i.e. in relation to America), the comparison is complicated further. And such complications can quickly multiply and choke any inquiry in its tracks unless some limits are stipulated from the start. Any sociocultural discourse normally demands such a delimitation, but it is particularly necessary where unexamined preconceptions dominate. Though what follows will try to cut through some of these difficulties, there is no substitute for a rigorous and systematic study of the two cultures. At this stage, only a general discussion is possible. In review, we may remark on a few features already evident in our discussion so far.

As the Gandhi-Nehru characterizations of the Indian culture and democracy indicate, India has produced so far a family of symbolic resemblance with the Western-style liberal democracy. India has a whole range of ideas about, and images of, an Indian democracy. Democracy is even publicly preferred, yet it is far from being an internal ideology in the same sense as in the West, and especially in America. India's democracy is formally powered by Western concepts, categories, and models of man, but informally, and more importantly, it is a contrast to the tradition in some contexts (e.g. as in caste, kinship, and marriage, see Chap 3) and yet in some ways familiar (e.g. as in diverse ways of managing friends, markets, and religion). Also, to India Western democracy is too familiar (as Nehru showed in his writings) to escape caveats and criticisms, yet still too distant to touch the entire life-style of the ordinary people. The Indian democracy provides forms to, and locations for, political and economic power but it still cannot channel, much less contain, the social functions, uses and meanings of democratic power. Hierarchy and inequality take charge there. Thus the people may challenge the democracy even as they "practice" it. The Indian intellectual also displays a similar schizoid approach to democracy. He usually has long conceptual criticisms of, and increasing empirical data on, the functioning of Indian democracy, but no systematic modern political philosophy or theory to "establish" (i.e., to interiorize) the case for Indian democracy, as if he feels no true need for it. It is as if a criticism of the Western models, and an allusion to the Gandhi-Nehru characterizations, can make up for such a gap. Symbolic connections

Culture and Democracy

are conveniently treated as conceptual and analytic relationships.

Even as we so observe, we have to accept it as a part of the modern Indian temper. India's incomplete or approximate formulations must be considered alongside the Western democratic ideology. Whereas the West increasingly puts its political-economic-military power behind its versions of democracy, India continues to treat democracy as an experimental form of formal government and power management. Yet India's democracy is far from simply superficial. For complex practical reasons, democracy suits India's cultural pluralism and inequality so conveniently that convenience creates reliance, and reliance an internal cultural justification and preference for democracy.

Notes

1. My approach to Tocqueville's study is obviously parallel to that of Dumonts' (1980: 13-20). If Tocqueville's assumptions, methods, and formulations concern two specific Western societies and their experience of democracy, they also *symbolize* much more. They offer a paradigm for a comparative study of democracy. As Tocqueville identified and characterized the fundamental properties of Western democracy, he also provided a sociology of egalitarian social order, and a window to logic of the equalitarian mind. Tocqueville is significant to our anthropological study for the above sociology and logic; as these properties arise from specific Western societies and their history, they also transcend the context of their origin. A symbolic approach facilitates such a wider reading; this approach does not let one become a captive of cultural uniqueness and historical particularism just to formulate ideological oppositions. Ideologies are not discounted but treated only as a symbolic configuration of values that influence, and get influenced by, the social reality as a whole.
2. While it is useful to recall the formulations sympathetic, by chance, to anthropological methodology and viewpoint, a systematic exercise remains in order. The goal of this essay is to show that such an exercise is justifiable and significant. It seeks to discuss cultural resemblances and representations available between the American (or more generally Western) and Indian democratic experiences, with primary emphasis on the latter. However, people's dilemmas, doubts, and limits will be integral to such an exploration; skeptical questions are as much a part of the contemporary cultural temper (intellectual as well as popular) as of the scholarship needed to develop studies of democracy as a way of presenting the multi-cultural experience.

The role of anthropological reasoning has hardly been pursued for showing how democracy tries to translate cultural differences, and how well (or badly) might it be able to do so. However, some tendencies may be expected: Anthropology generally reduces as it explicates intercultural differences. Approaching all differences neutrally and usually in a relative manner, anthropological analysis uncovers deeper shared sociocultural dispositions even as it compares values and distinguishes different forms of behavior.

3. A good example of ambiguity in Gandhi's use of Indian categories is *Rāmarājya* (literally Rāma's rule; ideal reign). Though he used it to stand for the ideal polity — everything and every person in their proper place, in proper significance, and at their maximum development — he was repeatedly misunderstood for a culturally specific reason: What to Gandhi meant a generalizable ideal represented only a Hindu ideal for his critics (e.g. see Bondurant 1965: 150-151). He had to explain this usage even during the last days of his life, though he had written much earlier that *Ramarajya* simply meant "Kingdom of God," and that "he acknowledged 'no other God but the one God of truth and righteousness'" (quoted by Bondurant). Such problems of cultural translation point toward issues only too familiar to anthropologists, although there may be no easy solution to such problems. However well universalized, a cultural idea or value always takes more after one cultural background than another. Even at best a conscious cultural explanation is not free of such a value slant; only it needs to be received and understood in the manner intended. Message receivers always play a critical role in translation. Hence the problem that dogged Gandhi remains before every anthropologist, every social scientist, and only better attempts, no final solutions, can be expected.

4. For Gandhi a core of moral values — truth, nonviolence, nonattachment, renunciation, and equality — matters, not political labels. Accordingly, he is often found seeking the same set of values whether he is commenting on democracy or socialism or communism (Gandhi 1959: 15-28). Whatever comes in the way of a pursuit of these values is rejected. He rejected "the essential selfishness of human nature" postulated by socialism and communism. Again, he observed:

> What does communism mean in the last analysis? It means a classless society — an ideal that is worth striving for. Only I part company with it when force is called to aid for achieving it. We are all born equal, but we have all these centuries resisted the will of God. The idea of inequality, of 'high and low,' is an evil, but I do not believe in eradicating the evil from the human breast at the point of the bayonet. The human breast does not lend itself to that means. (Gandhi 1959: 27).

5. Obviously, a cultural view of Indian democracy is a much more complex concept than what this discussion can include. Even the cultural roots of modern democracy in India are more entangled than

the Gandhi-Nehru formulations will suggest. Yet what they emphasize is indisputably a core of cultural themes and values. Their insights can be related to and traced historically back into the subcontinents' earlier values and practices concerning authority, power, and government, and they cannot be dismissed even within this larger picture. Ancient India's "village republics," assemblies, and councils inform Gandhi and his views on the role of *panchāyata* (i.e. the five-member administrative village council) in modern India. For earlier political ideas and institutions in India, see Altekar 1958.

An equally important point is that these Indian leaders, along with Tagore, Vivekananda, and Ram Mohan Roy, recognized (of course in essentials and in international terms) what Dumont has recently called logical and ideological "opposition" between democracy and hierarchy (Dumont 1967). But they did not, and could not, have stopped with its recognition. They experienced the juxtaposition of both in India and allowed for, as Nehru would say, "the change of function and even form to some extent" (1962: 19).

6. Since Dumont (1980, 1967) is the most recent anthropologist to have analyzed this issue for India, more comments are in order. As is evident from the above discussion, Indian leaders had recognized before Dumont a fundamental (i.e. ideological) conflict between caste and democracy. What Dumont can therefore bring to the subject is a systematic sociological understanding of the conflict. As an anthropologist, he would try to do so from both—Western and Indian— sides, for this step will help reduce what he calls sociocentrism. He indeed tries to do so, but with limited success, in my view, especially since all the recent (i.e. the nineteenth and the twentieth century) Indian ideas about and modification of democracy are excluded. Indian thinkers, ancient and modern, are selectively used (e.g. see Altekar 1958). Dumont finds democracy logically and culturally opposed to caste, and extends it, by implication, also to the entire genius of Indian culture and civilization. It is an ineluctable, total opposition. There is no place in his scheme for conflict *and* coexistence; it offers only ideological clash and annihilation. This is unfortunate and ironical, since he more than any other brought sociology and Indian thought together, and developed an anthropological discussion of critical political and economic issues of the time (Dumont 1977). Yet he must be firmly refuted (and at times rejected) whenever he overlooks, while discussing India, that Indian cultural perspective that underscores, despite conflict, values of tolerance, moderation, and accommodation. Without these, as Nehru had remarked (1962: 45-46), all material progress in India "may well turn to dust and ashes."

One consequence of Dumonts' methodology of ineluctable category opposition is that his discussion of Indian society and culture is quickly found to close on itself. As it explicates insightfully the hierarchical frame of Indian mind, it is found to be more interested in contrasting Western ideology than in a fuller study of the Indian society and civilization itself. This orientation is so intense and sweeping at times as to recreate a West-directed bias in his accounts (e.g. see Dumont 1966: 17-32; for a discussion of related issues by two Indian commentators, see also A. K. Saran 1962, and T. N. Madan 1966: 1-16).

CHAPTER 3

SOCIAL DYNAMICS OF INDIAN DEMOCRACY

Some critical forces of conflict and coexistence appear within the Indian family as tradition and democracy encounter each other. Sociologically, whatever is most significant must find acceptance within the family in order to secure a place within the cultural core. But normally family values are hardest to influence, especially in India, where traditional ways usually reign supreme and where all major socioeconomic decisions are made everyday. Thus if democracy has to mean something in India, it must register a positive influence within the family of the ordinary Indian. In my view this is the crucial test for Indian democracy, once it emerges out of political party headquarters, legislatures, courts, and local government office buildings. Accordingly, we will consider briefly the changing Indian social ethos, the issues of career and marriage, and a few critical interpersonal social relationships, as tradition and democracy test their strengths and weaknesses against each other, and against the changing socioeconomic forces.

India's family traditions remain pervasive and strong in many ways, yet they are neither a monolith nor a dead weight. They are a part of one's life, sometimes impregnable and sometimes highly vulnerable. Similarly, democracy in everyday life translates itself by social contexts and events; it has its own strengths and weaknesses and is neither foolproof nor invulnerable. For the society at large, democracy is not only a form of government but it is also a way of forming new ideas, hopes, and values. Democracy for Indians is a *different* way of thinking and "getting things done"; it is something to be reconciled with traditional ways and viewpoints. Such a reconciliation is usually gradual, selective, and even ambiguous. Yet contemporary India shows it in ample measure, both inside and outside the family.

Sociologically, modern democracy is a part of Western history and values, brought to India via the process of Westernization (especially see Srinivas 1966). Hence a discussion of social dynamics of democracy in India must start with issues of placement of democracy within Indian society, history, and culture.

Social Placement

As far as India is concerned, modern democracy has to appear in the context of the historical experience of the Indian Independence movement and its Westernized leadership. Equally importantly, it has to build upon the benign political, economic, and technological influence of the British Raj. The British started the process of Westernization in India in a dominant way and their political, economic, and legal measures created the basis for emulation and adaptation of the Western ideas and institutions. The same initiatives made modern education attractive, resulting in a new political and territorial consciousness that gave rise to modern nationalism. These Western influences persisted to yield momentous changes on the subcontinent; if the first produced the Westernized elite, the second carved out independent nation-states from the vast "British India." The germs of Western notions of economic competition, contract, and class also entered India to interact with moral status and world view.

The roots of Indian attraction towards democracy thus lie buried in the several decades of the last century and the early decades of this one. How they were being gradually translated and modified by the Indian leaders and elites has become a rich subject matter for social historians to systematize and interpret. For our purposes it is enough to recognize that the nineteenth century Indian reformers, political leaders, and intellectuals were foremost in critiquing and adapting Western notions of nationalism, nation-state, and democratic rule. They also deliberated on different versions of democracy, and as it succeeded or failed in different nations (e.g. Nehru 1981[1946]). Yet their primary concern was India. They examined themselves as they evaluated what the British Raj had brought to them.

A politically comprehensive, nationalist picture of India was raised from and nurtured in this soil. An underlying strain was:

Social Dynamics of Indian Democracy

India should try to incorporate only the best from the Western political, economic, and legal experiences; it should not, and need not, imitate them. Equally importantly, this incorporation should agree with the Indian society and history, and should respond vigorously to India's future. Poverty, overpopulation, communalism, political conflicts, and cultural diversity, all could be handled by India, it is assumed in this view, by popular participation, representation, open discussion, and consent.

This belief could be counted as perhaps the most significant triumph of modern democracy in India, for the Indian intellectuals and elites have predominantly kept their faith in and allegiance to the democratic norms ever since, providing the democracy a major justification in relation to the traditional Indian culture (whether classical or the popular) and its social organization (i.e. the family, caste, and village). The educated, urban Indian supports democracy essentially for the same reason as the vast rural population—to let people live as they want, without external, centralized control. When the political leadership intrudes too much, they may be rebuffed.

This fragile but congenial form of democracy, as appropriate sociological studies could demonstrate, has begun to influence the daily life-style, education, and expectations of the people. The influences have generally radiated from the urban centers, have changed their names and forms with context, and have touched most of the villages one way or the other. Elections, government, development, social welfare, administration, courts, and police— these are a part of the vocabulary of the working democracy in India. Politics, economics, law, technology, and education are the most visible domains where democracy is continuously being tested for its success as well as failures.

Democracy in India is a part of Westernization but it is not only that. It is also becoming Indian democracy. Yet the difference is feeble; the two remain intertwined. To discuss Westernization is to discuss a social context of Indian democracy, and vice-versa. Westernization in independent India has been increasingly heterogeneous in image and substance as the international contacts, technological advancements, and cultural criteria have multiplied. Now the British Raj experience exerts only indirect influences; the memory is fading. Among other "Western" influences are also those from the communist and socialist countries (but such considerations are beyond the scope of this discussion). Important for our purposes is the point that the images of American democracy and their influence, though a part of the larger processes of

Westernization, is most often grouped with the British version of democracy. Though inaccurate beyond a point, this linkage popularly persists. It is only strengthened further by the Indian Constitution, which, as already pointed out (see Chapter 2), is an amalgamation of the British and American democracies. It means that in India the two influences are now quickly and conveniently grouped together and treated "as just about the same." The strength of this popular perception cannot be overlooked, especially when juxtaposed to those for socialism in India.

This obviously has had a mixed result: On the one hand, it lets the British and American values of democracy ride on each other's back, while on the other it encourages the Indian to remain ignorant of the differences between them and to substitute one for the other for strengths as well as deficiencies. A similar point was recently made by Daniel P. Moynihan, when he observed that the Indians tend to treat Americans "as surrogate British with the transparently devious device of appearing to be generous . . . " (see *The Washington Post*, Thursday, July 29, 1982; p. A23).

However, it is also at such points that the role of popular social perceptions about America should neither be swept aside nor underestimated. The Indian and American channels of informal contact have increased and diversified in the recent decades. This is despite the fact the diplomatic and international relations between the two nations have remained distant and limited. The two cultures have developed sharing largely under informal channels and networks of communication. However, such a sharing is neither without obstacles and crossroads nor is it always well-defined and focused. Still, the fact remains that the American contact with India and Indians (in India as well as in the U.S.) has only increased in recent decades. More Americans normally visit India for various purposes, and more Indians come to the U.S. In terms of cultural presence, one could argue that the Americans have increasingly and rather imperceptibly replaced the British presence. They could do so easily not only since the two are popularly treated as the surrogates of each other but because the Americans number more and have greater resources for frequent visit, travel and study.

There are already relatively steady channels of informal cultural communication and exchange between the two countries. But they are almost entirely urban, hence greatly limited as far as India is concerned. Scholars, scientific and technological personnel, businessmen, and inter-agency government officials establish most of these channels on both sides, where the first two predominate and work largely outside the usual fluctuations in Indo-U.S. political relations. A stable pool of goodwill builds up especially among the educated of the two cultures as they visit each other's country and discover, underneath many visible (even irritating) differences, a similar democratic ethos and an undefined sense of shared similarity. Such visitors usually become messengers of such a sense once they return to their own country. They pass the images and anecdotes along. (The influence of newspapers and mass media is as peripheral and limited in this exchange as is those of critical intellectuals.)

Among the Indians it usually means encouraging relatives and friends to seek better employment and economic circumstances in the United States. It means acquainting them, reassuring them, and convincing them about what is better in America, the American system, and the American. Among the American counterparts it mostly means a greater appreciation of the enduring Indian culture, history, art, and philosophy; it means passing beyond the "elephant-Maharaja-snake charmer" picture of India on one hand, and seeing past the poverty-stricken begging Indian on a Calcutta street, on the other. Indians despair when Americans take so long to pass beyond these pictures; Americans despair when the Indians try to import to the U.S. their sociocultural and gastronomic markers based on Indian regionalism, sectarianism, and casteism. Each does not see what the other wants him to; each considers his culture and nation to be unique, with a unique message; and each is impatient with the other.

However, despite problems in cultural communication, or because of them, the effectiveness of informal communication continues to increase slowly between the two cultures. This increase may be undramatic, even imperceptible in the corridors of political power and public media, but it goes on. Whatever is good, bad or indifferent in each culture gets repeatedly evaluated through such a communication network. The two versions of democratic experiences and their strengths, claims, and deficiencies get evaluated against specific encounters and experiences. Onetime tourists, return visitors, regular travelers, and the long-term resident—all provide informal, face-to-face guidance about the "foreign culture." Indians residing in the U.S. guide other Indians essentially this way. Americans also inform and influence their countrymen, once they have been to India, through informal or formal channels.

Obviously, however, the zone of actual influence of Americans on Indians (or vice-versa) is much narrower, and among those

Culture and Democracy

influenced, only a few might take any concrete action (e.g. of travel, migration, and residence in the other country). Though it may be generally true that the Indian may tend to convert such an influence in a concrete step more than the American (who is economically more satisfied with himself than the Indian), the process of evaluation of influence is essentially similar with both the Indian and the American, and is often difficult for both. As far as the Indian is concerned, America offers a chance for better economic prospects, but it also means losing much of his sociocultural life. His American home is often home away from home; his social life with other Indians in America is a necessary but insufficient substitute. Only the second generation of the immigrant may try to do better in the host culture.

But such problems become easier as the information about the other culture becomes more accessible. An Indian in India listens carefully to a trusted person's experience. The next best thing to one's own visit is usually that of a relative, a friend, or an acquaintance. The Indian particularly searches out such an informal source of information; to him a travel brochure alone is seldom sufficient. The significance of such networks and channels for our discussion is that it is through them that several aspects of American democracy get communicated and are compared against the Indian's expectations and experiences.

An American going to India on business or pleasure now also increasingly depends on similar informal networks and evaluates their outcome essentially the same way as does the Indian coming to the United States. Both see the values of democracy in action in the host country and both compare what is similar as well as dissimilar to one's own. Both become social critic of the host country and both, more often than not, find some aspects that they sooner or later begin to appreciate or criticize about the other system. For the Indian in India, the American democracy impresses him with material rewards (i.e. food, clothing, technological gadgetry, cash savings, and generous gifting). The Indians resident in America usually carry these "goods" as they visit "home" on a more or less regular basis; their "things" speak about their welfare in the American society and the visiting Indian seldom downplays this "language" of American democracy. The Indian in India usually responds either with open appreciation (and a desire for emulation), or silent disdain and aloofness, or disapproval. The response depends upon the experiences of the Indian in question.

Such a diverse response of the popular Indian culture to the

American "exposure" is sociologically significant. It shows that one of the most obvious differences between the American and the Indian versions of democracy is found to be economic. Yet this difference remains ultimately superficial to the ordinary Indian. In America it is held primary. This difference is critical, and often a cause for misunderstanding. To the Indian his democracy, working under severe economic strains, faces many more challenges than does the affluent democracy of Americans. Equally importantly, there is also on the other hand the popular Indian perception that India and democracy go innately together irrespective of economic circumstances. It is so because the Indian cultural tolerance and social diversity find a democratic rule congenial. Obviously, however, such popular opinions are quickly controverted by the specialist, and the Indians themselves could be easily found debating them.

It is therefore sociologically important that the influence of democratic values—some specifically American and others generally Western—be traced through some concrete aspects of social life, particularly family. If the influences of Indian democracy are socially crucial, they must get reflected within the Indian family life in some observable form. They must either introduce additional considerations or modify and transform the existing ones. The democratic influences could not only be expected to conflict with the traditional norms. Viewed in terms of specific social contexts and their role in channelling democratic values in everyday life, the current Indian phase remains ambiguous, openly conflict-ridden, and wavering. But when viewed for the overall social direction during the past decades, the sociological impact of democracy on the daily life may be unmistakable in India. This larger impact may still be diffused and uneven (i.e. strong in some social spheres and weak in others), but it shapes the overall profile of the Indian social life in some critical ways, as we shall see.

Such a shaping hand is now visible within the family life. But I can remark here only in a preliminary way on this important subject. Concerned only with urban India, I will consider certain "central" and "peripheral" forces released primarily by the introduction of Western democratic institutions in India.

Career and Marriage in Modern Family Life

One important way to evaluate the impact of democratic values on Indian family life, especially in urban centers, is to focus on the critical issues of career and marriage. The two increasingly go together and influence other customary aspects of family life. "Career" symbolizes a family member's continuing expectation from self and society. It refers to available democratic avenues for education, employment, and social mobility; it stands for personal initiative as well as the available and realizable social opportunity. The considerations of a career link a family to democratic institutions and their rules germane within the surrounding society. Urban Indians now increasingly give priority to career because it is not only a major way to earn a decent livelihood but also to maintain one's social honor and position. If it is seen as a critical means for modern social advancement, it also translates as an asset in the traditional spheres of life: A good career these days ensures a good marriage (i.e. a marriage with a large dowry, and into rich and influential families).

This dual function of career is important to remember, for it shows how the forces of Indian democracy first converge on the richly coded cultural notion of "occupation" and then they begin to influence marriage decisions and family ethos. On the other hand, caste or family pride could also influence one's career, positively or negatively. The popular opinion is that one should give maximum importance to one's career if one wants to be successful in modern India, and that, unless careful, customary considerations could hold one back. Simultaneously, there exist lively and important cultural linkages between the two spheres. This property of the Indian system should neither be underestimated nor distorted when examining the impact of democractic values in India.

Pursuit of career and marriage constitutes a prime concern of the modern Indian family. Parents give maximum support to their sons (and daughters) so that they may educate and employ themselves better—better than their parents and immediate relatives. They should do so, among other reasons, to enable their parents to marry them better. Once well-employed and well-married, one completes a success story that others try to imitate. But if a "good career" does not culminate into a "good marriage," the success is considered incomplete, though perhaps less than when one has a "good marriage" but not a good career. Such evaluations of career and marriage are sociologically useful for understanding how the democratic forces for individual opportunity and social mobility actually work in the Indian society. But as the legal and political announcements of equality in India raise the expectations of those deprived and unsettle the fortunes of those privileged, the channels of new individual opportunity and social mobility are seldom free from social conflict. Actually, controlled social conflict has become a routine means for democratic change in India.

In modern India, one's bright career usually assures a better economic and social status for the family. Since a modern career is based on individual effort, on one's personal will to succeed, and since it cannot be passed along to one's progeny, the career-building activities encourage the Indians to develop a drive for personal success. Personal initiative is becoming important but it is still dependent on family, caste, and the influence of friendship. The effort often is to influence and modify institutions' decisions. Anthropologically, this is India's way to contextualize democracy, even if it produces ethical ambiguity and generates conflicting expectations. But despite such a trend, personal career-building activities in India introduce the individual and his family to some of those strains that characterize a Western society.

These strains now influence the family ethos and family lifestyle but seldom as completely as in the West. There are some conditions where the tradition still wins, some others where a seesaw test of strength goes on, and still others where the tradition has receded. The career and marriage concerns relate to all the three conditions. For the urban Indian, the priority of personal education and employment is increasingly unambiguous; the traditional order cannot now employ as many and as satisfactorily as it did in the past. The traditional occupations have not only lost prestige but are also found increasingly insufficient and inefficient at present. For example, not all available fabrics could be washed suitably by the traditional washerman (*dhobi*) anymore; dry cleaners are a part of the urban life; they give specialized service, earn much more than a washerman and enjoy greater social prestige. Displacements, even replacements, of traditional occupations are going on in urban India. Diversity, specialization, and mass production, all are increasingly encountered in occupational changes.

But equally often the "larger issues of life" are still found located in and guided by the customary goals and values. "Good" marriages for one's sons and daughters, for example, remain a clear goal for Indian parents; such marriages raise their expectations, hopes, and fears; and they count in the calculation of a family's income, expense, and savings. Having several daughters means that a father should earn more and save more to give sizeable dowries for marital happiness. But to be able to do so also means that their husbands must have a secure and promising career, for that is the means by which to move up in contemporary India.

Family members must now learn to seek an individual career (and a better paying job) from the surrounding new institutions. A traditional goal like "good marriage" must therefore depend increasingly on the issue of an individual career and its security under the democratic institutions and their values.

Such an interpenetration of democratic and traditional forces is characteristic of the Indian social situation. It also carries the imprint of the Indian ways of thinking and behaving as it lets the two social forces—status and contract—coexist and situationally prevail. If they subvert and corrupt each other in the process, it is popularly of little concern as long as they can serve the Indian sense of larger social propriety and moral purpose. Thus if a "good marriage" demands these days a sizeable dowry, then a good career secures more family income, better social position, increased incentive for individual earning and advancement, and culminates in increased savings for, and expenditure on, marriage. A better career, which symbolizes personal achievement, normally ensures a better marriage, especially for men. A sizeable dowry is not a ceremonial gift anymore; it is a definite economic transaction these days for the families involved. The traditional caste status is often insufficient to fetch a sizeable dowry; the status must combine with a good education and personal career in order to be fully effective.

I chose to emphasize career and marriage in the above discussion because they repeatedly draw attention to not only what is popularly found most critical to the urban Indian family life but also to the major issues of status, competition, and personal achievement in India. The career-oriented priorities change the profile of interpersonal relationships among the family members; they change the family ethos and world view. Let us briefly look into these.

Changing Family Relationships

Some of these changes are clear and firm, others only fickle, and still others hardly consciously recognized. Conceptually, the basic change is from the duty-bound family life to that based on competition and contract, respecting family members' changing individual rights and expectations. But within the family not only must the traditional and democratic claims negotiate but they should do so by respecting the feelings of one's near and dear ones. Here a dry ledger of one's rights and obligations does not suffice; customary attitudes, moral values, and personal sentiments also continue to count. Such a consideration therefore usually shapes the changes one notices in all the interpersonal relationships within the family.

For example, consider the changing paternal authority in India. Though Indian parents continue to be quite protective of their traditional prerogatives, there is a general relaxation under urban surroundings. The "unquestionable superiority" of parents, as Tocqueville termed it, stands muted when one's son, for example, seeks relative independence for pursuing his own career and ambition. On the other hand, one could obviously not say with Tocqueville that in India "there is in truth no adolescence," or that there is no domestic struggle as the parental authority changes its character under democracy. Today a son in India usually feels his way as he tests the limits of his parent's tolerance for independent behavior. The Indian father normatively abdicates his authority slowly as his son becomes a successful householder; the son's age and accomplishments are usually the primary criteria in such a transition. The democratic pressures are accommodated in this scheme essentially as a matter of practical affair. However, tempers flare and bad feelings linger whenever a father or a son rudely asserts his own rights, violating the implicit moral and sentimental bonds. No son is ever too old to do so. In contrast, in America, "the father has long anticipated the moment when his authority must come to an end, and when that time does come near, he abdicates without fuss" (Tocqueville 1969: 585).

Similarly, the father in American democracy "is only a citizen older and richer than his sons" (cf. also Varenne 1977: 51), while in India, a traditional society in transition, the father is an elder who still commands a distinct authority and respect on moral grounds. He is now of course also a citizen of the Indian democracy (and subject to its laws) but he is never merely an old citizen before his son (or the other members of his family). He remains the guardian representing the larger society and its moral force (cf. Tocqueville 1969: 586). He is the "elder" of the house, even if he and his son are two "equal citizens" before the law of the state. For if a father is cruel to his son, the cruelty could be either moral or legal or both. When it is legal, he commits a criminal act and the law takes over. Indian democracy thus imposes new limits on a father's range of social authority. But still there is ample room for his traditional authority to manifest, and to conform to legal constraints. Legally, a father loses all of his authority over a legal-age son; but since, in practice, the moral authority is seldom reduced to legal rights in

India, a father normally retains moral authority throughout his life. It is only when a law is broken and the court has to intervene that civil and legal equality makes its impact.

An Indian father's authority also rests significantly on what Tocqueville calls the "testamentary power." Comparing America with France, he noted how the American father kept his power intact, though this provision was less democratic (Tocqueville 1969: 585–588). In India the democratic legislations in the same area have either reduced or redistributed this power of the Indian father, but he still wields enormous customary authority for disposing of his property during his lifetime. His traditional moral position still dominates, allowing the impact of democratic laws to be slow and selective within the family. The father-son relationship may now be less austere, distant, and authoritarian in India than in the opening decades of this century, but it is still far from the situation where, as Tocqueville remarked, "a sort of equality reigns around the domestic hearth." Though one should not underplay the role of the change of attitude built into the traditional rules in India, the basis for the father-son intimacy, confidence, affection, and gentleness in the two (i.e. the Indian and American) cultures remains different. In America, according to Tocqueville, the basis lies in the "seed of equality" implanted within the father and the son; in India, it is fundamentally in the shared moral duties between the two. To an Indian adult, his father is an advisor; if he is closer to his father it is because his father voluntarily and affectionately lowers the curtains of social distance and superiority.

This customary locus and style of accommodation between the father and the son are, however, also congenial for facilitating practical partnership between the two. More often in everyday behavior than in observances, Indian fathers and sons illustrate such an attitude. The ordinary ceremonial barriers generally tend to erode faster when a father-son team launches a joint business or a professional firm. Still, however, there must always remain limits to this esprit de corps, for glaring ceremonial or moral improprieties can quickly wreck this fragile arrangement, even beyond repair. All "freedom, familiarity, and tenderness" must be expressed within such an implicit framework of respect and affection.

The position of women is also changing within the urban Indian family as the forces of tradition and democracy interact with each other. But compared to the father-son relationship, it is given secondary importance and changes are slower. Women acquire a civil profile as they receive higher education, seek a professional career, achieve socioeconomic security, and maintain these acquisitions *beyond* their marriage and family obligations. The last is usually the most critical test in India. Very often, as is popularly observed by men, a girl's education and career are to make her eligible for a good groom; both are usually a "gift" (even a part of the dowry) to the groom and his family, and the bride must normally be ready to give up her career if the groom's family or the groom so desires. To assert one's independence in such a matter is unconventional and rather unexpected even before an educated husband. A bride who seeks a career in spite of the husband's objections is thought to have brought shame to her parents and ridicule to herself. In contrast therefore to the situation of the American girl described by Tocqueville (1969:590-592), the Indian girl is still never left completely "to look after herself." The Indian women continue to seek traditional ways to protect themselves; it essentially means that she live with either her father, husband, son, or a close male relative. The most "emancipated" women today are those who pursue a prestigious career after marriage as a physician, administrator, and educator. Such a group may also include the most civic-minded, socially uninhibited, and "free." But even the emancipated women in India may not necessarily be anti-traditional or averse to family responsibilities.

A woman's position in the modern Indian family is most often kept tied to the concerns of a "proper marriage" and proper married life. The protective role of parents or husband is emphasized and the influence of her education and career must adjust to this criterion. She thus easily contrasts with the American counterpart. As a consequence, unrestricted social freedom for women is still regarded as immoral as well as "uncivil" in India. It is uncivil when whatever is traditionally immodest for the Indian women is also regarded as ill-mannered and impolite. This approach only proves the continuing deep influence of traditional etiquette on the Indian woman.

Politically and legally, however, she is a citizen equal to man; she can now inherit, vote, marry, divorce, and live independently under the protection of civil law. Whenever harassed by a relative, she can potentially claim her social and legal rights before the Indian courts. This legal picture of latent equality is composed and promoted by Indian democracy; it loosens the traditions surrounding her and adds a whole new background of redress. The sociological significance of this development should be correctly estimated. Though its social acceptance is still minimal, it opens a new avenue of significant legal security for women. It affects the Indian women of different social standing in different ways. To the urban uppercaste it mostly means a claim for equal opportunity for education and career outside the home. Legal provisions also provide additional and important avenues to seek justice when disputes arise in marriage and inheritance. Divorce is allowed. To the lower castes the scope of such provisions is wider and more immediate since they traditionally can marry more than once and attract disputes. Hence, to the uppercastes democratic legal provisions bring the court-enforced justice only as the last resort, and only when all traditional means fail; to those lower the same legal provisions apply more naturally, settling disputes and dispensing court justice. To have to go to court, for the uppercaste, means either a loss of traditional social esteem or, lately, a dubious leap toward Westernization. Law and traditional society still breed incompatibility in India.

The preceding changes within the urban Indian family show how Westernization and democratization relate to the traditional social order and its values. India is registering slow, uneven and ambivalent change. Given India's long social history and diverse culture, it could be no other way. Yet the change is revolutionary in significance. The Indian household genuinely reflects the vicissitudes of this silent revolution, for whatever matters critically reaches the domestic environs and whatever takes hold here alters the Indian culture. The general ethos of the Indian family in the post-Independence period, one could safely argue, is toward greater cultural openness, social mobility, and individual opportunity. Though it will be inaccurate to attribute all this change to a single cause, democracy, its role, explicit and implicit, should not be underestimated.

A social placement of Indian democracy is still difficult to evaluate; it is still too new and distant in some ways and too evident and untamed in others. The traditional and democratic institutions face each other everyday, releasing new expectations, conflicts, and compromises. At a more basic level, the traditional and democratic value systems are realigning themselves in a major way. My comments in this section concern some larger social issues. As we do so we move from the preceding discussion of specific contexts and changes to those concerned with certain overall configurations of values and perspectives. Yet the direction of change at both general and specific levels is interrelated; one illustrates as well as comments on the other. Accordingly, dilemmas of change for the Indian family illustrate and critique the interrelationships between values of caste and democracy.

From the vantage point of traditional India, democracy has already brought the genie out of the bottle. Caste ordained duties, transactions, and expectations face increasing conflict, fragmentation, disputation, and erosion. The caste system is exploited rather than followed; castes become groups for channelling rather than controlling politicoeconomic interests. Hence castes become "vote banks," and caste-ordained occupation and behavior a matter of practical convenience. "Vote banks" are a glaring contradiction in caste terms; they represent a political contract applied to all adults *equally* for ensuring uniform political participation and representation. The duty-based morality of the caste system is juxtaposed to politicoeconomic rights of the individual, with each exploiting the other by social convenience. Though castes initially guide and channel the burden of plentiful politicoeconomic conflicts, they tend to lose control of themselves increasingly with time, and lose sight of the larger moral system that shaped them. In other words, castes "disembed" themselves as they ostensibly "exploit" the popular politicoeconomic forces of independent India, and face erosion of, and serious breaches in the holism that they should represent.

Sociologically, therefore, castes lose their essence and vivisect their holistic experience as they chase democratic politics and its contrasting values. As traditional caste role clusters and their moral meanings lose cohesion and become insufficient for politicoeconomic goals, a "practical attitude" develops toward the caste order and its practices. This attitude encourages, for example, a politicoeconomic "profit-and-loss" view of social relationships. Demanding dowry at marriage, cornering power in politics, and converting position, power and authority into economic gains for one's family and relations are illustrations of this tendency. But as this goes on, something else happens: Caste members devise and condone unfamiliar, unprecedented, and even "unruly" behavior to meet the new range of demands on them. They try to "substantialize" caste *and* democracy together, but can do so only incompletely and face seething social enigmas and conflicts. As they discover old caste values and customs to be unsuitable, they make new caste ways indispensable in some ways but increasingly insufficient in most others. From the point of view of cultural ideology, these new ways are an untenable corruption of the caste order and its holism; they already represent an irreversible change of behavior and perspective, and they can move only away from the holistic idea and essence. Contemporary Indian castes are therefore only a shadow of their former type; unremitting democratic forces have robbed and depleted the caste system.

When viewed from the other—modern Indian—viewpoint, democratic politics and economics have faced changes at the hands of the Indian caste order and its persistence. This order "distorts" (or adapts) the egalitarian model of man to suit its own needs and conditions. Indian families show how this goes on everyday, giving ample evidence that democracy in Indian society cannot retrace the path of the West. India is already treating the democratic economics and politics its way and is getting significantly changed in the process. To argue that either India or the Western model of democracy can do any other way is to overlook the Indian historical experience as its recent reality. Yet India's version of democracy admits two relationships at the general level: It plays out the contradictory logic of hierarchy and equality in social life and enters symbolic negotiations with egalitarian cultural ideas and values. It is in the second context that some American cultural values and their popular images appear in India. We will consider some of these aspects in the next chapter in the context of the criteria for evaluation of democracy in India.

CHAPTER 4

EVALUATION, ADEQUACY, AND ETHOS

One of the distinct characteristics of Indian democracy at present is its ideological and social fluidity. Such a condition brings its own advantages to a study and they should be explored as fully as possible. Main advantages flow from the fact that democracy in India is still under social scrutiny and evaluation. It is in the process of "incorporation." Various competitive criteria of evaluation and adequacy appear in India to show how Indian culture and democracy examine each other from their distinct positions, and with their own strengths and weaknesses. In this important exercise neither Indian society and culture nor the Western democratic experience can be taken for granted; both sides have to prove their relevance to each other. Social experience tests any preconceived notions of superiority about the modern democratic order and its values. Actually, when looked from the Indian side, modern democracy, as a way of life (to use Dewey's characterization), must prove that it is more adequate than any other alternative in order to survive.

Democracy in India may be already passing through a range of criteria of justification, evaluation, and adequacy. But the scope of this essay will allow me only to give a sense of what is now relevant in such a domain of inquiry in India. I shall approach the issue with a view to develop a perspective on the passage of democracy in India, especially when democracy is approached as a set of popular notions and activities, and as a part of one's lifestyle. To the educated it may mean a "method of cooperative intelligence" (to employ another phrase from Dewey). An implicit argument of this essay is that democracy juxtaposes India to

America, another major democracy, not only politically and superficially but by social dispositions as well; this encounter encourages both sides to learn from each other's values and experiences. Directly or indirectly, American democracy represents a view of man and a major constellation of values that influence India in the later part of the twentieth century.

The following evaluations of and perspectives on democracy rest on the images, notions, and ranges of similitude that India has acquired essentially in this century, but especially after Indian independence. Reflections and images of American democracy participate in this acquisition but where they begin and end is difficult to ascertain. Actually, this question is not as significant as the fact that a whole range of analogy, adjacency, and similitude is currently evident between the two cultures, especially at the popular level. But if it is a fact that these images and reflections may only indirectly relate to the harsh reality of the ordinary Indian's life-style, it is also true that they are a part of the same social reality that democratic institutions in India produce as they release economic, political and legal forces directly affecting the ordinary person. A new model of man emerges from these forces, demanding new categories and criteria of social evaluation.

The Background: American Model

Let us briefly consider some defining aspects of this new model of man. We will employ it for comparison later on. American culture, according to an observer like Tocqueville, must reflect a new model of man shaped predominantly by democratic ideas and values. Such a model will form a basis for limited comparison with the Indian criteria and conditions. The American model is characterized by a core of critical cultural criteria concerned with self, society, and cosmology. I particularly draw attention to the cultural configuration provided by "nature," "competition," "individualism," "love," and "law."[1] They give the American culture a distinct content and profile. To understand them is to reach the cultural foundations of both American culture and American democracy. Each cultural category in this cluster relates with the rest in a cultivated polysemy. For example, the depth and resonance of such a category as "nature" in American culture is undisputed; Emerson wrote about it in the last century (1965 [1836]: 186-223) and included within it were his concerns about "commodity, beauty, language, discipline, idealism, and spirit." For him "nature always wears the colors of the spirit" (p. 190); "nature is the vehicle of thought, and in simple, double, and threefold degree" (p. 197). The same nature also shapes directly the reality of self, family, relatives, and friends (e.g. see Schneider 1969, 1980). Nature is heredity and innate dispositions in this context. Thought, reason, aesthetics and spirituality build on it rather than appear independently.

"Competition" is a fact of nature as well as a subject for rational thinking and just and fair social consequences. Open and just competition is integral to the ideal of American democracy and quest for all forms of social mobility. As Lloyd Warner (1962: 129-130) observed:

> The opportunity for social mobility for everyone is the very fabric of the "American Dream" ... It is the basic, powerful, motivating force that drives most of them [Americans] and makes all Americans partners in the well-being of each, since each feels that, although he is competing with the rest, he has a stake in the common good. When the principles of social mobility in the United States are not operating, there are troubles ahead not only for those who do not experience mobility but for every American.

The idea of social competition in America intimately related to individualism and equality (for an early and concise statement, see Tocqueville 1969: 503-513). But, as Warner had clearly noted (1962: 127-128), the principles of equality and of superior and inferior social (class) position produce an internal conflict, and both, "when balanced, are necessary for the proper functioning of contemporary American democracy." He also recognized that equality "is necessary to provide all men with a sense of self-respect and to establish the secular essentials of the Christian belief in brotherhood" (p. 128). Modern individualism fashions itself after this essential principle (see Dumont 1977: 15): "The evolution was from otherworldly individualism to more and more this worldly individualism ... " For America, as the modern Western civilization, "every man is, in principle, an embodiment of humanity at large, and as such he is equal to every other man, and free" (Dumont 1977: 4). Warner translated the same point in American democratic cultural terms:

> Americans—devout advocates of individualism—believe that individualism means that each man has within

himself the right to make his own choices and to make or break his life-career on the basis of his own judgments ... Whenever the American system of equal opportunity and individualism operates successfully and a man can make his choices and be rewarded when he does well, then Americans believe the system is fair, and their way of life is understandable to all because they can live and act as individuals and be rewarded accordingly (1962: 138-139).

The distinct American notions of "love" and "law" emerge from the preceding cultural foundation of nature, individual, and competition. Love is at once a multi-sided, deeply rooted idea and emotion with Americans. It is natural but not only a natural instinct. It is at once personal, social, spiritual, and intellectual. To be able to love is to be a complete human being, an individual, and to give and share love is to be ready to become lover and beloved, husband and wife, and parents and children. As Schneider (1980: 49) observed for American kinship:

> Love brings opposites [husband and wife] together into a single unit, while it holds together those things which are moving apart—the child and its parents, or brothers and sisters growing up, finding mates of their own, and founding their own families.... Marriage is for love, and forever, "through thick or thin, for better or for worse, till death do us part." It may *be* fun but it is not *for* fun.

Emerson's poem on "Give all to love" exalts the idea and feeling of love in a characteristically American way. Love stands for ever-widening meanings of self and of all that surrounds it. Walt Whitman, in his *Leaves of Grass* (1983 [1892]: 405), characterized in one poem America with nature, equality, love and law:

> Centre of equal daughters, equal sons,
> All, all alike endear'd, grown, ungrown, young or old, ...
> Perennial with the Earth, with Freedom, Law, and Love. ...

A recent community study by a French anthropologist emphasizes the point that this configuration of cultural values is neither idealistic nor ephemeral. Rather it is a part of the lived social reality. People are seriously engaged every day in seeking equality, love, individualism, and justice within the community they live (Varenne 1977; especially see part 3). Love is a part of their being and becoming within families, schools, churches, and communities. But when placed alongside law and government, love produces another range of conflicts and a democratic society must learn to resolve them by distinguishing *carefully* between law and emotion, and law and morality. To do so means to establish equality of all before law, and to let law become, as Oliver Wendell Holmes, Jr., the American jurist had said, "the witness and external deposit of our moral life.... When I emphasize the difference between law and morals I do so with reference to a single end, that of learning and understanding law" (Holmes 1960: 146). Political power is also expected to be constrained by a set of rules (e.g. see Walzer 1983: 282-284).

Both love and law locate themselves in life experiences and law always has to keep a delicate balance between logic, tradition, and customary values. Holmes put his finger on the dilemma law faces in a democratic society (1960: 153):

> The training of lawyers is a training in logic. The process of analogy, discrimination, and deduction are those in which they are most at home. The language of judicial decision is mainly the language of logic. And the logical method and form flatter that longing for certainty and for repose which is in every human mind. But certainty generally is illusion, and repose is not the destiny of man.

New Man in India

The preceding brief discussion of a critical configuration of American values is significant to our study. It highlights values of American democracy on one hand, and provides a version of modern man that Indian democracy variously reflects, on the other. At present India is negotiating the abyss found between the status and contract-based social orders. The duty-bound Indian is increasingly facing the competitive, market man on one side and the scientific-rational man on the other. Simultaneously, these three men are freely politicizing themselves, both within and without the bounds of democratic order. With familiar rules of social life changing fast, the Indian social reality is betraying a perplexing heterogeneity. It is increasingly difficult to explain by customary formulations of kinship, caste, and community. Social perplexities arise because values of tradition and democracy clash daily, demolishing or realigning centers and boundaries of people's actual roles and statuses.

A common way to characterize this Indian condition is to say that it is "complex." But what does it mean? For our exercise, complexity essentially means two things. First, as already mentioned, India now encounters at least three distinct but simultaneously interacting models of man—duty-based man, market man, and scientific-technological man. As they compete and jostle for attention within the family and in the wider society, they produce unresolved or incompletely resolved conflicts and doubts. As erosion of traditional centers, boundaries, and ranks deepens such doubts and ambiguities, an incomplete familiarity with or alienation from democratic values introduces uncertainty still further. People doubt the old as well as the new, the near as well as the distant. Even they may begin to doubt their own ability to sort things out.

Second, social complexity in India translates into some identifiable relationships, particularly those of intensity, intricacy, variability, and ambiguity. Value conflicts between tradition and democracy readily illustrate these dimensions of complexity. Popular, democratic politics has intensified the quest for power and profit in old (i.e. caste) as well as new (i.e. adult franchise) terms. As the traditional centers and positions of power have become empty and as the democratic institutional centers have only imitated the actual power, the chase for the *satisfying* position, power, and authority is evident throughout India. Diverse groups and individuals are intensely power and position hungry. But whatever transitory power and position one corners takes much effort and strategy and usually means little because in such a scheme as one gets more one covets more, and the more one seeks stable power the more elusive it becomes. Hence the twin feelings of insufficiency and dissatisfaction never leave that new Indian within whom social duty, competition, and rationality churn but only halfway in an ethos of uncertainty and ambivalence.

Intricacy in the modern Indian condition acquires distinct character and form as intricacy does not simply stand for elaboration and complication but for personal and group uncertainty (and hesitancy) as well. Similarly variability does not refer only to cultural, linguistic and regional diversity in India but also to varying inconstancy and inconsistency in ideas and behavior. In

Evaluation, Adequacy, and Ethos

the political arena intricacy and variability thus acquire strategic significance; they help keep the other side guessing. But to manipulate such a complexity for highly practical, short-range goals is also to yield to unexplored and unknown perplexities in the long term. As the new Indian manipulates this complexity he may get manipulated in return in some highly unsuspected ways. The larger perspective is easily lost when power is found manipulating politics and politics power every day for trivial as well as momentous reasons. Normative values, laws and ethics all become a fair game for manipulation in such a context, and a politician or a practical man shifts his attention from inspirational to managerial goals, with justifications derived from practical circumstance.

Democratic politics in India is doing some unexpected things to power, authority, legitimacy, and law. It questions traditionally domesticated power around family, kinship, caste and village; it lets the traditional power run wild and creates new centers of power, often raw and untamed. As democratic politics does all this, it also encourages the Indian to redomesticate power as a citizen and a rational market man. The Indian thus finds himself in a whirlpool of change, essentially at the mercy of untamed, often capricious and ad hoc centers of power and authority. Wild power not only disrupts the notions of moral and jural authority but it also puts on deceptive appearances. Promise and performance, ends and means, and rhetoric and meaning—all diverge with wild power, and produce inconsistency and confusion. But politically such inconsistencies become "strategic," and all kinds of strategies are justified in politics. Thus in India "caste," "region," and "language" are well-known strategic political resources. But they domesticate power only in appearance. In fact, they become conduits of raw power running from individual to individual, with little control over rules of the actual game. In such a circumstance caste, region and language may do one thing in appearance but quite another in fact. For example, while they may seem to be domesticating democratic power, authority and legitimacy, they end up being pawns of untamed power. Such a picture remains incomplete, however, until we add that whirlpools of untamed power also suffer from participants' deep-seated hesitancy, uncertainty, and doubts. Such a power nexus exploits (and depletes) itself as it exploits centers of authority, legitimacy, and law.

Democratic India encounters not only untamed power, unkept promises, and a doubting public but it also inculcates new attitudes toward power and authority. Ideally, democracy must abhor authority and decentralize power. A person with too much power should feel guilty and be a cause of concern and suspicion. Power cannot be legitimized for its own sake, since it must reside in public consensus, serve a public interest, be justified in such terms, and, most importantly, yield just and fair social consequences. But these notions must contend at once with Indian criteria for legitimation of power—personal age, honor, kinship and caste status, and positions of authority. However, these criteria do not channel as much as upset and rearrange the legitimacy and conduct of power by public consensus. And as the Indian criteria do so, they ironically violate and subvert themselves and their moral criteria of legitimation. They act outside their *dharma*, becoming anomalous to both Indian tradition as well as democracy. Thus all proper criteria of legitimacy face a crisis, a doubt, and an uncertainty.

Yet the deeper the crisis of legitimacy, the more is the yearning and need for legitimacy. It is also a point recently discussed by Habermas and Dahrendorf (1979: 109-111) for Western democracies. Whether in India or the West, questions of "justice of power" loom large in various ways. For India it is not simply a case of conjecture; a pervasive crisis of legitimacy is at hand. Both traditional and democratic institutions land one "in a cage of bondage" (as Dahrendorf will say, "with an expectation that there is much that might happen, but does not happen," and with "doubt in the legitimacy of their [the elites'] power" (Dahrendorf 1979: 111). A vital consequence of such a crisis is that law must also reflect a similar uncertainty sooner or later. The role of law in Indian society and democracy is a complex subject of study itself (e.g. see Derrett 1968; Galanter 1971, 1972, 1978, and 1981). Indian laws, modern court-enforced and indigenous, are diverse but persistent; they support democracy one way and exploit and deform it another. Modern law courts in India, though pervasive and reticulate, spur but cannot complete democratic change in India. Many other factors—traditional, economic and political—intervene, each with its own justification, leaving modern law with a critique of the Indian society on one hand, and a self doubt on the other.

Thus if Indian democracy is throwing up its own quandaries on all sides, it is neither unexpected nor unlike the experience of the West. The Indian, who tries to roll into himself at once the duty-based perpetual Indian, the competitive market man and the scientific-technological rationalist, blurs models and meanings of modern man in daily life. He selectively shifts, displaces, mixes, and ejects cultural contents of the traditional as well as the modern man. He ejects morality from democracy and traditional authority from power.

Shifting Values and Meanings of Man

India and the West forge a resemblance as they practice "pluralist" democracy and seek improvements in its effectiveness by increasing people's participation in it (for a concise discussion of these developments in political theory, see Macpherson 1977: Chapters 4 and 5). Largely unconsciously and haphazardly, India, like the West, has increasingly regarded democracy first as "simply a mechanism for choosing and authorizing governments, not [as] a kind of society nor a set of moral ends; and second that the mechanism consists of a competition between two or more self-chosen sets of politicians (elites), arrayed in political parties, for the votes which will entitle them to rule until the next general election." India has increasingly ejected that ethical and moral content from democracy that the Freedom Movement had awarded and that Gandhi had injected with a distinctly Indian content. He saw a natural kinship between *swaraja* ("self-rule") and democracy, and democracy and the pursuit of non-violence, equality, and individual freedom:

> True democracy or Swaraja of the masses can never come through untruthful and violent means, for the simple reason that the natural corollary to their use would be to remove all opposition through the suppression or extermination of the antagonists. That does not make for individual freedom. Individual freedom can have the fullest play only under a regime of unadulterated *Ahimsa* (Gandhi 1947: 10-11; originally *Harijan* May 27, 1939).

Contrasted to this view of democracy stands the late twentieth century model which, as Macpherson (1977: 79, 81) points out, holds that "democracy is simply a market mechanism: the voters are the consumers; the politicians are the entrepreneurs." This model essentially takes after the economic man and his sovereignty in the marketplace (for an early and influential study, see Schumpeter 1947). The proponents of this model of democracy "see the citizens as political consumers, with very diverse wants and demands. They all see competition between politicians for the citizens' votes as the motor of the system.... [But] they differ somewhat in their views of the extent to which it also provides some measure of political consumers' sovereignty."

To the Western political theorist the implications of such a shift are enormous. It may mean, in some senses, as Macpherson argues (1977: 1-2), the demise of "liberal democracy," especially when "liberal" stands for "the democracy of a capitalist market society (no matter how modified that society appears to be by the rise of the welfare state)." Whether such a drastic conclusion is premature or not, is a question for political scientists to study, especially after the evidence is in from the last two decades of this century. To an anthropological study, the above shift conveys several interrelated messages at once: First, there is now skepticism about the viability of liberal democracy even among those who gave it birth. Second, democracy, like other social ideas and institutions, must undergo significant contextual modifications and cultural refigurations as it fares through the history of the Western and non-Western societies. Third, democracy cannot be expected to remain aloof for long from people's everyday ideas and actions (because it will be against its own tendency to acquire ever wider, egalitarian participation and representation). Fourth, democracy, in spite of its internal strains, is fundamentally concerned about "a model of man" and its reflection in the actual lives of a people while tackling the issues of power, wealth, and justice. Fifth, thus though largely implicit when it goes to any non-Western society, democracy is always about two considerations at once—a value configuration standing behind the democratic model of man, and plans of action for collective participation and representation and its ethical justification.

All the above characteristics are congenial for an anthropological study of democracy in different cultural contexts. Such a study may now be necessary and unavoidable, especially when liberal democracy, as a politicoeconomic theory and a popularly justifiable life-style, is at crossroads, facing conflicting pulls of human history. While the fuller course and consequence of the recent dilemmas of liberal democracy are buried in future, an anthropological study of culture and democracy can neither ignore them nor could it be satisfied only with a favored, West-limited viewpoint. However pervasive, and however universalized, Western democracy, in anthropological analysis, offers only *one* of the several possible approaches toward a just polity. In such a view liberal democracy, though a result of a specific Western historical circumstance, allows different societies and nations to develop it according to their own genius and social condition. Yet the assumption is that different societies will be inclined to recognize and preserve its liberal core—a model of man intrinsically disposed to equality and personal freedom.[2] Simultaneously such a hope is tempered with the realization that a democracy's dilemmas, doubts, and fragility arise from both within and without. Democracy, not unlike science and technology, is that product of Western history and culture that is also capable of being easily misconstrued and misused.[3]

So approached, culture and democracy become a rich and varied field of inquiry for political anthropology. Cultural relativism (for the anthropological tradition, see Hatch 1983) helps explain the essential role of sociocultural variability in democracy. But it does so by injecting skepticism into certainty and variability into "monolithic" perspectives. As Macpherson's discussion makes clear, political theory may gain especially from it at this point in history when the survival of liberal democracy depends on what different peoples and nations in the world *mean* by "that liberal-democratic ethical principle—the equal right of every man and woman to the full development and use of his or her capabilities" (1977: 114).

The model of man in Western liberal democracy rests on the value of the "equal right of self-development." Macpherson (1977: 48) puts it in anthropologically sensible terms:

> The root is a model of man . . . [who is] capable of developing his powers or capacities. The essence is to exert and develop them . . . The good society is one which permits and encourages everyone to act as exerter, developer, and enjoyer of the exertion and development, of his or her capacities.

This characterization rests on the idea of equality, a value patently conceived and developed in the modern West and launched in terms of the concept of "individual" (e.g. see Dumont 1965; Lukes 1973). On capacity, Isaiah Berlin (1978: 102) provides a valuable comment:

> Equality is one of the oldest and deepest elements in liberal thought, and is neither more nor less 'natural' and 'rational' than any other constituent in them. Like all human ends it cannot itself be defended or justified, for it is itself that which justifies other acts—means taken towards its realization.

In other words, equality is a value of values for liberal democracy. Even when taken across the Western–non-Western divide, this is the value democracy defines itself by. It may be translated, adapted, modified, and deformed but it should neither be formally rejected nor totally absent, if democracy has to be genuine. Hence, whether a Western or non-Western case, here is an ideological measure against which all the twists and turns of different national experiences are evaluated. As far as the major shifts of the Western democracies are concerned, Macpherson's four models summarize them not only reliably but, as shown by my commentary alongside, they also provide certain key cultural constructs and their formulations. In anthropological language Macpherson's models encapsulate the historical experience and offer a cultural critique of democracy in the West. His models represent variations of the same theme identified above—a quest for equality and the approximations of an appropriate model of man.

Macpherson's first model, labelled "Protective Democracy," for example, incorporates a vital sociological shift: "Thus there is a sharp break in the path from pre-liberal to liberal democracy. A fresh start was made in the nineteenth century... The earlier concepts of democracy... had rejected class division, believing or hoping that it could be transcended, or even assuming that in some places—Rousseau's Geneva or Jefferson's America—it had been transcended. Liberal democracy, on the contrary, accepted class division, and built on it" (1977: 23-24). In India liberal democracy was shaped first by the ideas of such similar-yet-different national architects as Gandhi and Nehru and then taken up (more realistically) by major alignments of traditional caste, communalism, and regionalism. The democratic ethics of equality and an economic view of man and society have slowly but clearly moved to the center of the new Indian politics. But these new goals instigate as well as suffer at the hands of new politics—a politics that deconstructs the tradition as well as modernity to develop its own character and course in India.

Such a shift is sociologically critical for India. It puts money, market, and competition between the traditional man and the larger society. As Dumont (1977) will say, Indians thus begin to forge relationships with "things," putting things between interpersonal relationships. Liberal democracy started in India without a conscious examination of the following assumption: "The founding model of liberal democracy took man as he was, man as he had been shaped by market society and assumed that he was unalterable"

Evaluation, Adequacy, and Ethos

(Macpherson 1977: 43). Democracy in India, therefore, encountered most of all the problem of governing what in Macpherson's model would be "inherently self-interested conflicting individuals who are assumed to be infinite desirers of their own private benefits." The rules of the new game were thus set for the Indian after independence. His duty-based view of himself and of the larger society were challenged and debased; his traditional economic relationships and moral motivations became deficient rather suddenly (especially when viewed against the long-standing Indian social history and culture).

A caste member became a voter overnight but what this "leap" entailed took much longer to manifest before the society. It meant "first, that democracy is simply a mechanism for choosing and authorizing governments, not a kind of society nor a set of moral ends; and second, that the mechanism consists of a competition between two or more self-chosen sets of politicians (elites), arrayed in political parties, for the votes which will entitle them to rule until the next election" (Macpherson 1977: 78). The "leap" also meant that "democracy is simply a market mechanism: the voters are the consumers; the politicians are the entrepreneurs.... Not only did the market model seem to correspond to, and hence to explain, the actual behavior of the main component parts of the political system—the voters and the parties; it also seemed to justify that behavior, and hence the whole system" (Macpherson 1977: 79). The Indian must, accordingly, learn not only to become a voter and a self-chosen politician but also to organize political parties that compete with, and oppose each other to govern and regulate the flow of all major goods and services. The entire society in this development becomes a political arena as well as a marketplace, both superimposed and mutually competitive, and both challenging the traditional models of man and moral order.

Obviously, the Indian shift is more complex than this, for the tradition has responded to such challenges with its own vibrancy and creativity. Most of all, the tradition entraps democracy within a web of symbolic language of "national cultural" ideals and images. Both politicians and markets depend on this rhetoric to make sense of themselves, and to discover new ways to approach the voter. Tradition and democracy in India are therefore locked in quite a skillful combat and alliance; they explore and exploit each other by context, each learning to cope with the other's improprieties and forwardness. The tradition learns to live with the morally objectionable "marketeer" (*bazāru*) and political opportunist while

Culture and Democracy

democracy must recognize the enormous reality of caste hierarcharchy, familial bond, and religious emotion.

Today's India draws on a third shift as well. It concerns the Indian scientist and the intellectual, who represent the West-inspired rational man and rationality. As specialists, researchers, and observers they concern themselves with issues of widest and most critical nature. They concern themselves not only with the form and future of democracy but of self, society, natural order, and mankind. The scientist is sure of himself, perhaps too sure (e.g. see Uberoi 1978); the intellectual is a bundle of qualified ideas, values, and social conditions, and of skepticism that yields to larger doubts (e.g. see Béteille 1980). Whether both reside in the same person or not, they represent a rationalist world view and approach that *modern* democracy does not (and cannot) ignore. Simultaneously, the state and marketplace constrain scientists and intellectuals. A democracy demands just and equal availability of opportunities for educational and intellectual development, but the factors of unequal wealth, power, and privilege intervene as surely as do the forces of market demand and supply to let the issues of social justice assert again.

Modern India is full of this multisided, multivocal confrontation and contest. But the hidden message is more significant. It is investment in, and certainty about, the rise and triumph of rationality sooner or later. The India of intuition, emotion, and empathy is somehow found deficient and unsuitable (just as the traditional morality is found to be) when tactic, strategy, contested rights, monetary profits, and "scientific outlook" reign modern India. Not unexpectedly, democracy discovers an ally in rationality; both spring from the same cultural soil, giving substance and shape to each other; both justify and explain each other in relation to human experience. Yet democracy and rationality also make a tenuous and implied connection with India's cardinal cultural values—tolerance and moderation. As long as such a connection survives it helps both tradition as well as democracy. It also lets reason and reasonableness stay together. But the eighties find this connection under unprecedented strain. In such a circumstance, all sides lose, giving way to endemic conflicts and emotional wounds.

Criteria of Evaluation

Democracy in India is thus under a critical and diverse examination. It is being tugged and pulled in several dimensions at

Evaluation, Adequacy, and Ethos

once. The situation demands that Indian political theorists and thinkers subject democracy to as thorough an evaluation as the traditional values and practices. Democracy came to India as a form of government and as a historically conjured up, incomplete social experience. Not unexpectedly, therefore, tradition and democracy discover each other's weaknesses. Neither works perfectly in daily life and neither can claim intrinsic superiority, unless one set of value assumptions is favored over another. When looked from the ordinary Indian's view, democracy has to prove its bona fides in terms of a host of social criteria. I shall simply mention some of these (leaving out any detailed consideration at this point) since they consider democracy from the ordinary person's point of view, a topic of anthropological concern.

As I have discussed in another context, Indian social groups, even the lowest, engage themselves today in identifying, articulating, and evaluating new ideas and activities against practical concerns (Khare 1984). For the ordinary man, except for periodic election campaigns and voting, there are limited conscious and systematic occasions for identification of what is democracy and how does it work. In this amorphous ethos, identification, legitimacy, and evaluation of democratic ways acquire much greater immediacy but are equally hard to learn. Trials and errors of daily life are the only reliable educators for the common man. They present a ground-level perspective on democracy, accompanied with hopes as well as frustrations. The ordinary Indian juxtaposes the traditional to the democratic to resolve the extremely practical problems of food, clothing, housing, health, and employment. What works in relation to these issues matters more and more, giving a more convincing legitimacy to democracy than any theory could. But when democracy in India works this way at present, it is still quite uneven. It brings limited protection to only some weaker groups; it stops far short of the promise. If it may be still considered better by some than the earlier British order, such a claim could be easily disputed by those whom the caste system bestowed a stable position and privilege. To these democracy is a perversion of established justice and fairness.

Any close evaluation of Indian democracy must therefore vary with social position and circumstance of the people. Generally, democracy has worked to redistribute hereditary positions and privileges but has succeeded only partially. Still the underprivileged entertain the hope of doing better, increasingly challenging the privileged. It is a development of singular significance in the

Culture and Democracy

Indian context, though it also means increasingly intensive challenges, differences, and conflicts between different social groups, and a greater rise in inequality rather than equality, and dissimilarities rather than similarities. These are to be sociologically expected when as intricately ordered a society as India tries to rechannel the status, power, and authority coursing in the age-old institutions into those democracy has recently legislated. Questions of cultural legitimacy, popular justification, adequacy, satisfaction, and certainty enter increasingly into the Indian's mind as he finds himself caught into the conflicts and gaps between the old and the new. These are the criteria for evaluation of Indian democracy; they are relevant to the people as well as to the analyst.

As Macpherson (1977) notes for the West, questions and criteria of adequacy dominate the passage of democracy in India. They also apply to all the foregoing criteria of evaluation. Hence in today's India the issue is not whether democracy has acquired any cultural legitimacy and popular justification but whether it is adequate (i.e. satisfactory and sufficient) to meet the challenge of Indian conditions and values. Adequacy also draws attention to the issues of the appropriate and the inappropriate, especially in India. For example, democracy still does not apply equally to all sectors of social life in India, (e.g. kinship and marriage), and by definition it should not (and cannot) force itself on the people. If it does, it immediately loses its legitimacy and popular credibility.

Essentially, three types of adequacy concern the Indian democracy most and they translate in analytic terms as experiential adequacy, justificatory adequacy, and explanatory adequacy. To people democracy should be adequate for practical reasons and as an improvement over past living conditions. This adequacy should also be such that it secures better moral, legal, and cultural justifications for democracy. Hence if a caste member obtains his education and employment within democratic institutions and is able to secure food, housing, clothing, and safety for himself and his family, he finds democracy adequate for practical purposes. But since this practical effect of Indian democracy is neither always assured nor equally satisfying to all, such consequences do not translate simply into increased justificatory adequacy. Except for politicians and political analysts, very few ordinary people justify democracy in so many words. People regard democracy either as coterminous with government (*sarkār*) or leave it to those heading the political and administrative machinery. What such a view means is important: Democracy acquires implicitly the same legitimacy and justificatory adequacy that Indian government has earned so far — it is context-dependent; it is always conditional and often contested among politicians.

But democracy is always a topic of popular discussion. While the political parties and governments treat it variously as a polity, power tactic, and political expediency, the ordinary Indian evaluates his experiences. People routinely characterize the modern government and its institutions in order to judge how government stands up against the politician-preached democratic ideals and expectations. The greater the gap between the political promise and performance, the greater is the general inadequacy discovered in politicians, and the greater is the feeling of dissatisfaction with current state of affairs. In such a situation the criteria of sufficiency and satisfaction are very hard to discuss, except in terms of the degrees of tolerance of insufficiency and dissatisfaction on the one hand, and sporadic instances of sufficiency and satisfaction on the other.

If anything, the ordinary Indian has shown, so far, a remarkable tolerance for gaps between political promise and performance. He has endured dissatisfaction and insufficiency without doubting the basic goodness of democracy. This is because he does not easily equate inadequacy with insufficiency and insufficiency with dissatisfaction. His inclination toward cultural tolerance and diversity nurtures his sympathy for democracy. Both produce a fortuitous adjacency within modern Indian politics and society. But sociologically nobody could take this situation for granted. The question whether tolerated dissatisfactions could not explode in India is increasingly vital to ponder, especially once a major crisis overtakes the cultural reasonableness and sensibility of the people. Much more than an academic argument (i.e. between resiliency and polarity) is at stake in the current interrelationships between culture and democracy in India. The people are riding a roller coaster with their own deep hopes, doubts and fears, and the roller coaster is mostly a dubious creation of undomesticated power politics and politicians.

This a good point to reflect briefly on a critical issue implied in the aforementioned discussion of the criteria of evaluation: changing meanings of social and political power in India.[4] As I have already remarked, relationships of status and power, status and contract, and duties and rights are undergoing a major realignment in modern India. But any realignment implies not only relocation and revaluation but also dislocations and devaluations. Again caste and democracy illustrate the issue well for India. As the institutionalized caste structure of status and power is required to realign itself with the democratic counterpart, dislocated power and devalued moral authority come immediately into view. The disenfranchised caste rulers and landlords in independent India clearly illustrate what Dahrendorf calls "undomesticated power" (from the viewpoint of a democratic state). Similarly the legal and civil rights of a son as an individual devalue the traditional moral authority of a father, especially when he is old and economically dependent. Such instances of dislocated traditional power and devalued authority (from the traditional society's viewpoint) have tended to increase alongside the increased legitimacy, economic value, and glamor of political power and politics. The consequence is unrestrained pursuit of political power.

If traditional India subdued (or domesticated) law, politics and economics by a moral order and world view, modern democratic India has increasingly "de-linked" all three first from the moral world view and its authority, and then from each other. However, de-linked law, politics, and economics compete to overtake each other. Whereas economics dominates politics ever more in the West, law settles disputes on legitimate "rational" grounds and conditions to disallow total dominance. In modern India, politics dominates economics and society at large; law is still too weak to fend off endemic politics and nebulous, hidden centers of undomesticated power. India's dilemma is not only India's; it is rather a far more fundamental question:

> Since his [Weber's] time, and to the present day, a wide social aspect of the domestication of power has been uppermost in people's minds: How can one prevent the translation of sectorial power, in industry for example, or the military, or the secret service, into political power? How can the rational legitimation of power be extended to all society? And how can one make sure that an eminent position with respect to social status, an aristocratic name, a very high income, is not abused for the illegitimate exercise of power? (Dahrendorf 1977: 125).

Misplaced and misused power is of great concern to a democratic state because it can easily subvert its core ideal values: from equal individual rights to self-development, basic civil liberties, legal equality, and popular sovereignty. But as Western philosophical, sociological and political theories amply point out, equality is a complex hope—a social expectation largely free from domination, or as Walzer (1983: xiii) will say, "no more bowing and scraping; fawning and toadying; no more fearful trembling; no more high-and-mightiness; no more masters, no more slaves." Democratic power of the state is expected to protect a modern society from the traditional modes of dominance and domination exactly because state power "guards the boundaries within which every social good is distributed and deployed. Hence the simultaneous requirements that power be sustained and that it be inhibited, mobilized, divided, checked, and balanced" (Walzer 1983: 281). Checked and balanced political power allows a society to follow "the principle of giving as many people as much as possible." It puts the pursuit of equality as an idea in a distinct way: "Equality [is] desirable because men are different, and in order to enable people to be different in their own right rather than at the expense of, or at the mercy of, others" (Dahrendorf 1977: 122). Within such a scheme, equity and social fairness stand at the heart of legitimate political power, and checked and balanced (or domesticated) power at the center of the complex hope for equality.

Modern India's main struggle, in comparison, lies in limiting the range of actual social inequality, and narrowing the cultural zone of "justifiable inequality" (as Dahrendorf would say). But this must be done while democracy must do what it does elsewhere—raise people's hopes for equality and seriously entertain claims for eventual equity and fairness. These initiatives—simultaneously legal, political, and economic—demand that the Indian assert himself as a democratic citizen and that equality of opportunity translate into equality of result (as he quotes Daniel Bell, see Dahrendorf 1977: 128). Not unlike the West, modern India also places at its center a demand for economic equity. But the greater the hurdles in its realization, the sharper is the sense of frustration and the more the longing for promised results.

Such a condition only intensifies questions about the legitimate use and meaning of political power. The more the politicians employ their political power to curry political favors to clients and associates, the more enigmatic and distrusted does the political power become for the public at large. And such political power—undomesticated, misused, and anarchic—points toward a generally fragile confidence in democracy to cultivate political power. Undomesticated power can quickly rip apart the social fabric of a democratic state, since, as Walzer points out (1983: 281), "Political power protects us from tyranny ... and itself becomes tyrannical. And it is for both these reasons that power is so much desired and so endlessly fought over." India is experiencing all this anew, even if power struggle is nothing new to its diverse culture and history; democratic use of power is at once attractive as well as alien to the Indian politician. Wielding public-invested power is new and attractive but its controlled use is still alien and peculiar.

The modern Indian process of redomestication of political power needs to be studied anthropologically. For dislocations of the traditional power structure are as important a part of this process as are the untamed uses of both old and new (democratic) networks of power and authority. The conception and meaning of power in Indian life is fast changing. The politician is both cause and consequence of such a change. As a political leader, he mixes and matches old and new networks to suit his immediate purposes; he exploits rather than controls political power. Power means "getting one's own way" and holding on to and augmenting one's position (i.e. occupying a *kursī* or *ohadā*). A democratic control of undomesticated political power (i.e. redomestication of power) is still precarious. But the attempts are afoot and such an exercise is usually subject to diverse social pressure—local, regional, and parochial. Only the major formal institutions of the national government may withstand such forces better. But the institutions in India, as elsewhere, ossify too easily and social forces change too quickly to allow one seriously to redomesticate power. It is a major task for any society. India is simultaneously going through the need for legitimate power and the crisis in legitimate power (cf. Habermas in Dahrendorf 1977: 111ff).

The limited scope and purpose of this essay does not allow any further analysis of political power as a vital criterion for the evaluation of Indian democracy. But the significance of the issue is obvious. In order to justify itself, democracy has to evolve a culturally credible and reliable network of political power structure up and down entire India. It is a huge exercise by any criterion and India is fully dramatizing it its way. Real-life hope and despair are as integral to this drama as are the everyday confusions and bafflements of the ordinary Indian. Even his natural tolerance and moderation are taxed as widely as perhaps never before. There are increasingly fewer truly apolitical, noncontested social or personal spaces left to withdraw oneself into. This confirms, among other things, that the politicoeconomic individual of the West (see Dumont 1977) is being born with difficulty from the womb of democracy in India. Is it an expected but dubious consequence for India? Perhaps.

Dilemmas and Doubts

As any specialist on modern India knows, much is going on in India rather simultaneously, heaping complexities on complexities. A mere awareness of this "problem" forces the specialist to identify a specific manageable area of inquiry and a congenial theoretical perspective, and settle with these for a period of his intellectual life. This is what I have done in my research; little more. Yet, on occasions, more general concerns of the time intrude persistently, changing the safety of a specialism. Larger dilemmas and doubts of the actual life demand as much attention as hidden structures and meanings. Current interactions between Indian culture and democracy make a similar demand, for dilemmas and doubts are a part of the same "reality" that helps the specialist argue for his preferred models and explanations. I shall briefly allude to certain dilemmas and doubts that surround modern democracy in India and elsewhere. To do so as a major theme of the essay is appropriate: Dilemmas, uncertainties and doubts represent the modern temper in a critical manner, especially toward the end of the century. As a product of contemporary social conditions, these properties attach themselves to Indian tradition as well as democracy. Even a comparative study of democracy faces certain dilemmas, which, beyond a point, can be neither dismissed nor ignored any more.

An anthropological study focuses on comparison. It can therefore neither confine itself to just one case of democracy as being the perfect example nor close itself to alternative ideas and experiences of divergent societies in pursuit of democracy. For these reasons alone anthropology must attempt a comparison of democracy between such diverse societies as India and America. But this way anthropology also draws attention to a basic issue: A discussion of Western democracies, however thorough, cannot predict and guide diverse global translations of democratic idea and experience. Even when informed by the Western democratic experience, different peoples should be expected to approach democracy in the context of their own cultural values and history. Thus democracy needs to be studied not only as a political ideology but also as an accepted total life-style, as an attempted and incomplete social experiment, and even as a symbolic nod. The anthropological perspective assumes that peoples' diverse socioeconomic backgrounds and goals shape democracy in actual life. Relative successes and failures of actual life guide most people most of the time, even if we grant that democracy attracts so much attention today as a political ideology. Anthropologist's neutrality arises from this perspective; he attempts neutrality for important intellectual reasons, even though he may be imperfect; he relies on cultural relativism but is not an absolute relativist. As he interrelates ideas and actions he also ranks them to provide better interpretations and explanations. And as he does all this, he often discovers dilemmas and doubts surrounding certitude, yet sense amidst quandaries. To do so is to encourage full discussion of a complicated subject.

Democracy and modernity are such subjects. They implicate each other as each helps define the other. Products of the rational mind, they become a commentary on the limits of the rational mind itself as they fare through the changing world history. Moreover, dilemmas and doubts about modernity cast a shadow on democracy, and vice-versa. This close interrelationship is important to recognize because it is as integral to the modern intellectual temper in democratic societies as is a deepening skepticism. Self-doubts exist within both democracy and modernity. Both represent human options, choices, chances, and alternatives, but both may doubt themselves as the human conditions get complicated. As Dahrendorf (1977: 35) observed:

> Every one of the motive forces of modern societies has produced its own contradictions; and at times it appears as if these forces are no longer capable of dealing with their effects. More growth does not remove unemployment, and more equality does not overcome the frustrations of citizenship.

Dahrendorf's proposal for dealing with what he calls "contradictions of modernity" is to control individualism of the West by promoting "ligatures" or linkages alongside options. "Ligatures are allegiances" to, for example, "forefathers, home country, and community" and "life chances," another of his conceptions, "are a function of ligatures and options" (see Dahrendorf 1977: 30-39). This is a way to control what Robert Merton called long ago the "cultural chaos" inherent in modern societies (see Merton 1957). Dahrendorf does "not want to criticize modernity, but I want to show that it creates its own problems and in that sense encounters boundaries which are beyond guilt and repentance" (1977: 120).

Evaluation, Adequacy, and Ethos

Yet Dahrendorf is sensibly cautious about "the themes of [modern] history since they are not connected either by a straight line or by a dialectical pattern or by any other rigid logic of development" (1977: 120). Democracy and modernity, in my view, amply illustrate this qualification; both are history-bound categories of the West and try to remain so when transported to non-Western cultures.

However, dilemmas must appear before both democracy and modernity when, for example, the ahistorical Indian confronts them with his approach to events as moral episodes, interrelated by a moral cosmology and world view. This illustrates what I call the "intrinsic dilemma" of a cultural system. Such dilemmas arise when the fundamental values, ideologies, and perspectives of one cultural system conflict gingerly with that of another over a period of time. People's deep-seated cultural dispositions are concerned here, including definitions of self, society, and ultimate values. Though they do not change easily, they relate and respond to changing social conditions and practical (i.e. legal, political, and economic) goals, the stuff of which "extrinsic dilemmas" are made. Extrinsic dilemmas concern such affairs of daily life as earning a decent living, maintaining one's social status and honor, and contesting and competing for wealth, power, and authority. Extrinsic dilemmas are considered superficial and transitory while the intrinsic ones persist as a riddle of life. To the Indian mind democracy not only brings both dilemmas but each dilemma also feeds on the other.

Modern man's dilemma is how to remain parochial and universal — both at once. Therefore, "whenever we lay bare an idiosyncrasy of the modern mind, we make a little less impossible the task of universal comparison" (Dumont 1977: 9). Modernity in India suffers from the same schism. It remains too West-centered in India to establish a meaningful dialogue with the traditional culture. Since the word "Western" is still assumed to stand for all that is universal, superior, and rational (which is best exemplified by the rise of science and technology), the traditional knowledge and insights are separated, devalued, and treated condescendingly. This way the modern Indian remains alienated from the core of his own culture, complicating any genuine reproachment and understanding between tradition, democracy and modernity. The Indian is deeply ambivalent toward the West. This way the Indian is also unable to gain a genuine perspective on the West to understand himself better (for the value of the reverse process in anthropology, see Dumont 1977: 9). Hence modernity creates and maintains its own blindspots and its own dilemmas because, as Dumont points out (1977: 10), "modern man, closed in upon himself and perhaps misled by his sense of superiority, has some difficulty in grasping his own problems." What is useful to remember in this context is that modern man had assigned the same blindspots to the traditional man in the fifties.

Dilemmas of democracy in India, therefore, cannot be resolved without a serious and honest understanding of tradition and modernity in each other's terms, and in the context of total society and culture. In a country like India, modernity is no longer new or dispensable, whereas tradition remains its backbone and essence. Now India can neither return to some pristine, traditional condition nor can it fare in today's world without its own integral and distinct identity. India shows that it wants to remain Indian in essence and style as it becomes modern by discovering strengths and weaknesses of modernity (see Singer 1972). Though all quandaries of democracy cannot be attributed to modernity (nor viceversa), the two cannot be considered separately for a non-Western country like India, and problems of one segment reflect on the other. And unresolved strains and dilemmas between modernity and democracy, and between these two and the traditional order, tend to increase social problems in unpredictable ways. Unless political thinkers and leaders devise appropriate steps to reduce strains, people are left at the mercy of social events for unconscious and haphazard responses to deepening dilemmas. Unresolved dilemmas introduce uncertainty, uncertainty raises new doubts, doubts cause misunderstanding, and misunderstandings produce social distrust, strain, and even spontaneous violence.

While there is no place here to discuss this chain of social dispositions evident in India as democracy and modernity interact with the traditional culture, the role and meaning of doubts and uncertainty cannot be passed up without comment. Rising but unfulfilled expectations, more competition for scarce goods and services, and hidden political motivations of others—all introduce doubts in interpersonal relationships. Customary certainties give way to the uncertainties of a changing and wayward society that promises more than it can deliver. More critically, doubts cast shadow on vital constituents of the society—centers and symbols of legitimacy, justice, satisfaction, security, and hope for survival and progress. Doubted power cripples the powerful as well as the ordinary citizen; both lose selfrespect; and the more they lose it the more they conflict with each other as adversaries to regain it somehow. As Walzer pointed out, "Citizens without self-respect dream of a tyrannical revenge" (1983: 310).

In India the situation is more complex. The traditional notions of self-respect (i.e. via personal honor, caste status, and kin appreciation) have clashed with those of democratic citizenship, without any clear goal, policy, or plan. The ordinary Indian therefore finds himself increasingly powerless in both the traditional and modern sense. "Deprived permanently of power, whether at national or local levels, he is deprived also of this sense of himself" (Walzer 1983: 310). The modern Indian begins to doubt himself as well as those who symbolize legitimacy and authority. His doubt verges on cynicism, with a deepening crisis in interpersonal confidence. Such a doubt deepens still further once power and wealth are allowed to corrupt each other. "Citizens without money come to share a profound conviction that politics offers them no hope at all. This is a kind of practical knowledge that they learn from experience and pass on to their children. With it comes passivity, deference, and resentment" (Walzer 1983: 310-311). Modern India, like America, shows a similar sequence of social dispositions. If anything, these dispositions are too evident. They are still raw and the society did not have the time (or the plans) to resolve underlying political and cultural strains.

India's unconscious approach to democracy is sociologically complex and its perplexities are very real. Dilemmas, doubts, and quandaries—all crowd the contemporary Indian. Simple contrasts and oppositions between India and the West do not do justice either to the Indian tradition or to the sensibilities of the Indian. Even with best efforts, such accounts tend to distort, misrepresent and misjudge the social reality in different degrees. In order to reduce this problem, first, democracy must be seen in the full context of a people's society, history, culture and world view, whether the discussion concerns a Western or a non-Western country. Second, people's values, meanings, and perspectives must be taken fully into account for their clear rules as well as ambiguities, doubts, and dilemmas. That even a political philosopher can treat such anthropological properties centrally is shown by Walzer (1983: 314):

> One characteristic above all is central to my argument. We are (all of us) culture-producing creatures; we make and inhabit meaningful worlds. Since there is no way to rank and order these worlds with regard to their understanding of social goods, we do justice to actual men

and women by respecting their particular creations. And they claim justice, resist tyranny, by insisting on the meaning of social goods among themselves.... To override those understandings is (always) to act unjustly. (Walzer's parentheses.)

India's many strains and quandaries in modern times arise when political leaders and the Westernized elite "override" people's popularly shared meanings and sensibilities to enforce their own views, preferences, and societal models of democracy. Normally any gap between the leaders' and people's sense of a situation is routinely attributed to people's ignorance and to leaders' greater insight in people and social events. But this may not be always so clear. The situation may sometimes hide an insight-crisis in leadership. Since democracy follows the pulse of the people through its political leaders, any serious gap in communication between the two can directly affect the role and meaning of democracy. Such a gap can delude the leaders and confuse the people. Leaders can misread and misjudge people's intentions and their capacity for sensible ideas and behavior, and can overestimate themselves as they set out to remove people's confusion, doubt, and ignorance. To accept such a possibility for contemporary political leadership may not be a sign of its weakness but only a necessary recognition of the social complexity that leaders must today grapple with. Any simple and sure sense of superiority vis-a-vis people may be resisted and examined rather closely. When people of a society suffer from wide-ranging dilemmas and doubts, its leaders, unless discerning, cannot remain far away from them. Demands for better leadership tend to increase in the same proportion as old guards misread people's pulse and their *status quo* power structure fails them. An atmosphere of uncertainty engulfs the people, whether elite or ordinary, and the gap between leaders and the people continues to widen, eroding tradition, democracy, and modernity — all at once.

There is another perspective for as large and complex a democratic society like India: It demands too much from its leaders and leadership organizations. India must evolve a different notion of leaders and leadership, more suitable to realigning social forces — religious, political, ethnic, and economic. A know-all charismatic leader may be increasingly impossible. For, as Dahrendorf (1979: 135) noted, "We are living in a world of uncertainty, in which nobody knows all the answers, and those who claim they do cannot prove that their answers are right." Less presumptuous leaders who like to stand by the side of the people, not above and away from them, may be useful. Moreover, India is only too painfully aware of moral regression in public and private lives. As it showed with Gandhi, it responds most to genuine moral appeals and still seeks true moral progress in everyday life. Such a sense of the Indian is neither arcane nor merely a run, once again, toward his traditional-spiritual cocoon. His sense, while nurtured in the Indian context, agrees with those of others. For example,

> That there is a case for moral progress seems to me much less doubtful; the imperfections of human society are painfully obvious at a time which seems to have come full circle from the precarious existence of primitive life through modernity and civilization to new threats to the survival of the human race (Dahrendorf 1979: 134).

Democracy in India plays a fragile but multisided role with the Indian and his sensibilities. It raises hope and uncertainty together for the deprived and the ordinary; it challenges the old privileged groups one way and affords them political and legal avenues to protect themselves in another. Democracy challenges traditional ways and values but often only selectively and for politicizing religion. Hence as it erodes the traditional morality, and as its own values remain trapped in legislatures and law courts, the people sense a wider moral regression, a widening gap between promise and performance, and a deepening uncertainty.

Yet hope has not left them; even the severely deprived Untouchable hope and strive. (For a study of this ethos among the Indian Untouchable, see Khare 1984). Encouraged by democracy, the Untouchable view the traditional caste system from the outside, much the same way as does Walzer for making a point about the scope of justice and "complex equality" under social differentiation: "Viewed from the outside, from our own perspective, the Indian Brahmins look very much like tyrants—and so they will come to be if the understandings on which their high position is based cease to be shared" (Walzer 1983: 315). Indian democracy erodes this sharing but again only incompletely to let dilemmas, doubts, and suspicions grow between the Brahman and the Untouchable, the quintessential representatives of social privilege and deprivation in India.

The current dilemmas of the Indian are thus clear. They are as much of the contemporary Indian condition as of tradition and democracy, and of modernity and the modern world. No simple and easy blames can be assigned anymore; there are no more sure and certain patent cures for complex human—national and international—motivations. Interrelationships between culture and democracy amply illustrate these larger issues of the times, whether one is concerned with a preeminent democracy like America or a striving and clamorous one in India. If democracies working within different cultural backgrounds learn to communicate with each other, they may perhaps understand better themselves and the call of times.

Notes

1. Attention may be drawn to those anthropologists who worked on the American society and culture to provide a comparative frame of cultural reference. Some did it consciously, others only unconsciously. I find Lloyd's Warner's (1962) writing helpful, especially when he is commenting on American culture in general. He did American sociology anthropologically, providing useful insights on American values and behavior. The next generation of American anthropologists grew up with an explicitly comparative theory of culture, and turned their other-culture experience to study their own culture. Milton Singer (1972) and David Schneider (1980) represent it well for us. Singer started with American studies, went out to conduct field research on the Indian civilization and returned later to American culture and semiotics (see also Singer 1984). Singer prepares the way for my study, but my interest involves a different sequence. I may interpose any implied or explicit study of American society and culture within an ongoing research on India. Such a step allows me to study not only another view but also to appreciate those who study India as American specialists.

   Schneider's analysis of American culture is useful to me once again (see Khare 1983), and this time far more explicitly. His treatment of "nature," "love," and "law" is clearly insightful and rich, allowing an outsider like me to relate it to the formative stages of American culture and world view. My discussion tries to build on this contribution in various ways in this as well as the other chapters of the essay.

2. This presupposition is not easily upheld either in theory or in the practical world. Obviously, the Western theory of democracy faces a genuine dilemma. If it lets each nation have its own version of democracy, it may mean admitting too much of diversity and losing that value core—a model of man with equal rights to self-development, before law, in civil liberties, and in political voice. If the theory resists such a move, it may be contradicting its own postulates of liberal

democracy for open and unforced choices. As Macpherson (1977: 9) pointed out: "The definition of the [liberal] model depends on value judgements about what *are* the essentials, and those judgements cannot be defended merely by invoking a definition" (Macpherson's emphasis).

How could the presupposition be, then, justified? Perhaps only by an intrinsic cultural sympathy: Peoples once exposed to liberal democracy will incline themselves toward a similar, even overlapping essence of "human freedom" and "good society" as they develop their *own* governments. All the roots of such a convergence will have to reside in human capacity for mutual respect and reasonableness, ensuring, as Macpherson would say (1977: 115), "a strong sense of the high value of the equal right of self-development."

3. This is a limited parallel. For example, as technology can be misapplied and misused not only within but outside the West, but without any direct blame on the "producer," democracy also remains, like any other cultural product, capable of deformation and misuse. It can also disrupt a system already in place, and without providing a better and more acceptable alternative. Though democracy is premised on consent and alternative options, it can also weaken and disrupt those avenues already working within an alien society. These points have, of course, direct relevance for India as a longstanding society, and as a developing nation. Democracy brings its own uncertainties to India, even as India discovers its own cultural weaknesses.

4. As I have done throughout this study, I shall comment on the issue from two perspectives—the people's and the specialist's, showing interrelationships between them as necessary. This is integral to an anthropologist's approach, and its significance may become evident when anthropological discussions are compared to others. For more comments on the subject, see next chapter.

In order to illustrate better some of my concerns on the subject, I shall focus on two recent discussions of political power. I refer particularly to Ralf Dahrendorf's (1977) discussion of political power and associated issues in *Life Chances* (see particularly Chapters 4, 5, and 6; pp. 96-140), and to Michael Walzer's (1983) treatment of the same topic in *Spheres of Justice* (see Chapters 1, 5, 11, 12, and 13; pp. 3-30; 129-164; 249-321). As I refer to these two scholars, I am particularly aware that they are neither India or South Asia experts nor do they wish to apply their observations to developing countries. Perhaps they should be more significant to us because of these properties. Since they do not wish to constrain their observations by the third-world complexities, any resemblance or similarity discovered should be less affected by the tendency to construe locally the criteria and values of democracy.

CHAPTER 5

CONCLUDING REMARKS

To be concerned with a comparative anthropological study of tradition and democracy in India vis a vis America is to examine the familiar as well as the unfamiliar almost simultaneously. It is a challenge to anthropology to demystify the familiar and the intimate rather than the exotic and the remote. India and America provide a particularly appropriate exercise in this regard. Democracy is still a new dimension of life in India, while it is familiar and intimate to America. On the other hand, Indian anthropology has been almost exclusively used to studying peoples and cultures of the subcontinent, while American anthropology focused more and more on other peoples and cultures until very recently. The seventies saw a change in this disciplinary configuration: American anthropology returned home to a definite extent to give more attention to American society and culture. The eighties continue the trend.

Comparatively, India, which has one of the largest cadres of professional anthropologists, has turned its attention to developmental problems in contemporary society and culture (including those urban, rural, and tribal). A discussion of tradition, democracy, and modernity in India extends the same direction of research, but much more directly and critically than the usual social change studies. To study democracy in India means to study closely the comparative Indian and Western criteria of experiential adequacy, justificatory adequacy, and explanatory adequacy. Indian anthropology, in my view, is now prepared to investigate these beyond a general identification of forms, functions and processes of modernization and Westernization. Though this is not the place to argue this point directly, with further supporting evidence, the present exercise provides contexts and reasons for proceeding in such a direction. The ongoing exchanges between Indian tradition and democracy should be examined not only for sociologically critical reasons, but also since they raise issues of widest public good, safety, and survival.

This exercise has taken the view that (a) democracy in India has to prove its suitability within a holistic cultural system and in competitive political arenas; (b) democracy, encoding Western and American values of modernity, equality and justice, encounters the rich and resilient Indian tradition in myriad forms and forges complex (i.e. intricate, intensive and often conflicting) interrelationships with it; (c) tradition and democracy increasingly face the critical questions of appropriateness and adequacy for independent India, and democracy has to prove itself under diverse social conditions, without any special favor or inherent superiority; (d) the Indian democratic exercise is in search of social legitimacy as it critiques and realigns the old centers and boundaries of power, authority, social privilege, and individual worth; and (e) it seems that democracy must fare through a dilemmatic, confusing social phase in order to evolve an Indianized version, with assured experiential, justificatory, and explanatory adequencies. Such a course for Indian democracy seems sociologically unavoidable but whether it will be successfully completed or not is still hidden in the future.

Issues of justice, fairness, "complex equalities" (and inequalities), and new self-definitions are a central part of the Indian exercises on "distribution of citizenship," to use Galston's (1980: 278) phrase. More people show a tendency to question the traditionally given as well as the politically promised. They raise questions of evaluation and adequacy for traditional as well as democratic institutions and their representatives. But then they face a deep ambiguity. In this situation the dissatisfied "play politics" as a corrective measure while the privileged do the same to retain or augment their position. Politics becomes an end itself especially when it not merely mediates and distributes power but attracts dominant wealth, perquisites, and positions to politicians. Instead of redomesticating power in appropriate institutions, such politics treats power "strategically" for its own perpetuation. It feeds on undomesticated power, using strategically even people's declining trust in political power and the powerful. Notions of justice and fairness also stand the danger of being politicized in such a circumstance. In India it yields, first, alienation of the traditional norms of justice; second, separation between law and morality; and third, aberration of the estab-

Concluding Remarks

lished notions of both traditional and democratic justice by untamed and avaricious politics (for a wide-ranging discussion of law and morality in anthropology, see Geertz 1983).

The general ethos such developments produce in India is unmistakably evident. As observed before, it is marked by dilemmas and doubts. This ethos is a subject relevant for anthropological analysis but certain precautions are necessary. Foremost, the ethos should be viewed in terms of certain underlying sociocultural processes and their significance. (If it is viewed in only immediate terms and through daily events, the larger sociological implications may be missed.) So approached, the general ethos of Indian tradition and democracy betrays dilemmas for both. Indian tradition finds itself constrained today in new ways as democracy awards voting to all adults and makes every adult a citizen with certain inalienable legal, political and economic rights. Similarly, democracy faces the challenge of a classic hierarchical society and its system of moral justice. The cultural distance between the Indian tradition and democracy is still so much that even the best circumstance must allow for some skepticism. In fact, as unresolved dilemmas accumulate in India today, usually aided by avaricious and untamed politics, skepticism gives way to doubts, doubts to suspicions, and suspicions to interpersonal distrust directed both ways—toward traditional and civilian roles and relationships.

Such attitudes characterize the Indian ethos simultaneously but unevenly. They form a part of the social reality and, in anthropological terms, represent some realignments during the ongoing clash and accommodation between tradition and democracy in India. It is as if this way old power centers, value categories, and behavioral boundaries modify themselves and accommodate those established by democracy. It is as if sharp value conflicts and differences entail emotional stresses and the people have to go through them to change their values and world view. India is going through this psychosocial exercise in a pervasive manner at present. Its internal social conflicts and cultural doubts must be related to, and evaluated for, the configuration of deeper ideological values. Skepticism, doubts, dilemmas, and quandaries emerge when people discover the familiar to be ineffective and the unfamiliar necessary and powerful (even if tentative). The familiar traditional ways suffer from a loss of certainty in such a circumstance yet people find modern ways more immediate and controlling. They also prepare themselves somehow for change, hoping that it will be for the better.

India demonstrates all this as a part of social reality, and some more. People critique modernity also by context and circumstance, and their initial attraction to it becomes slowly qualified. Not only that, the fading traditions may reassert themselves as ethnic or communal religions (usually in a revivalist form), while modernity continues to promise more than it can deliver. Thus comparative identifications, evaluations, and accountabilities become necessary and give rise to a "strategic mind" (which even the lowest—the Untouchable—in India now show; see Khare 1984). People tend to lean toward whatever works in practical terms, whether it draws on traditional schemes or modern or both in some combination. Still this practical approach to one's life's events does not resolve all issues, especially questions of ultimate values and meanings. The longing for moral certainty and a predictably secure life remains. Whenever it is frustrated and the demands of the practical world overwhelm, people feel puzzled and concerned. Both Indian tradition and democracy amply yield these conditions at present.

In this essay I have tried to identify some social forces—cultural, social and political—which give rise to dilemmas, doubts, and quandaries in modern India. Beginning with a rationale for juxtaposing democracy to culture on the one hand, and America to India on the other, the essay focuses attention on democracy as a comparative sociocultural experience. Whether weak or strong, or poor or rich, diverse nations of the contemporary world must learn to view democracy this way and be prepared to learn from each other's experience. This is perhaps the only sensible, and anthropologically defensible, way to view democracy and to let it find its due outside the geohistorical specifics of the Western world. This is also the way to move beyond captive democracy. Peoples' diverse movements to secure rights and voices across the globe test the advantages as well as the limits of liberal democracy, and in this way it is already a global cultural heritage. But the question whether the outcome will always be nearer to the Western models, expectations, and experiences may be irrelevant after a point. People's cultural background is sure to be reflected in the definition, content, and direction of any popular democracy.

The essay substantiates this proposition in India as it examines briefly hierarchy, power, family, personal career, and marriage. Viewing these in general and specific terms allows us to see how democracy is faring in India, showing its approach to American and Western models and meanings of man. The resulting picture is

Concluding Remarks

striking but neither for ideological clarity nor for simple confirmation of the Western experience. If anything, India depicts how democracy must be challenged with seething conflicts, and how it must be constantly evaluated for adequacy and satisfaction. Sociologically, India is involved in a life and death struggle of the hierarchical man on one side, and the egalitarian man on the other. The struggle is likely to be prolonged and tumultuous but indecisive (and unspectacular) for a long time. Both models of man will bend and modify. Such signs are already there and both may (or may not) modify themselves beyond easy recognition. But there is no simple retreat now for either Indian tradition or democracy. Even as the Indian politicizes his own region, religion and culture in order to evolve and incorporate a "strategic democracy," India, as a moral and cultural entity, faces unremitting (and perhaps unprecedented) centrifugal pressures.

Much is thus happening to the Indian culture these days. Religious, political, and economic differences assert themselves in the name of democracy, often yielding unstable and incomplete alienation. This is because democracy can neither prevent social differences from appearing nor can it afford to let them go unchecked beyond a point. Indian culture supports such a disposition. Thus if coalitions and compromise try to contain political strains, moderation and tolerance try to restrain traditional religious, regional, and cultural divisions. But either one or both can fail, putting Indian culture and democracy to their severest test. Once such a possibility is kept in front, the social function and meaning of cultural ambiguities, middle grounds and doubts become evident. To live and work through these domains is to keep the possibility of cultural moderation and tolerance alive. But when India opts for total and complete value polarizations, India will not be the same India known for so long. For it will have lost its holistic vision. Then it will be an India in search of a new cultural anchor. But whether India completes such a polarization or not,

> We must know that, as, through science and commerce, the realization of the unity of the material world gives us power, so the realization of the great spiritual Unity of Man alone can give us peace.
>
> Rabindranath Tagore (1970[1922]: 130).

REFERENCES

Altekar, A. S.
1958 *State and Government in Ancient India.* Delhi: Motilal Banarsidass.

Berlin, Isaiah
1978 *Concepts and Categories.* New York: Penguin Books.

Béteille, Andre
1980 *Ideologies and Intellectuals.* Delhi: Oxford University Press

Bondurant, Joan V.
1965 *Conquest of Violence.* Berkeley: University of California Press.

Bowles, Chester
1969 *A View From New Delhi.* New Haven: Yale University Press.

Brecher, Michael
1959 *Nehru: A Political Biography.* New York: Oxford University Press.

Burns, James MacGregor
1978 *Leadership.* New York: Harper Colophon Books.

Coomarswamy, Ananda K.
1978[1942] *Spiritual Authority and Temporal Power in the Indian Theory of Government.* Delhi: Munshiram Manoharlal Publishers.

Dahrendorf, Ralf
1979 *Life Chances.* Chicago: University of Chicago Press.

Derret, J. D. M.
1968 *Religion, Law and the State in India.* London: Faber and Faber.

Dumont, Louis
1965 "The Functional Equivalents of the Individual in Caste Society." *Contributions to Indian Sociology,* No. VIII, pp. 85-99. Paris: Mouton and Co.

1966	"A Fundamental Problem in the Sociology of Caste." *Contributions to Indian Sociology*, vol. IX, 17-32.
1967	"The Individual as an Impediment to Sociological Comparison and Indian History." In *Social and Economic Change: Essays in Honor of D. P. Mukherji.* Eds. V. B. Singh and Baljit Singh. Bombay: Allied Publishers. pp. 226-48.
1977	*From Mandeville to Marx.* Chicago: The University of Chicago Press.
1980	*Homo Hierarchicus* (Revised Complete Edition). Chicago: University of Chicago Press.
1983	*Essais Sur l'Individualisme, Une Perspective Anthropologique Sur l'Ideologie Moderne.* Paris, Seuil. pp. 46-47.

Emerson, Ralph Waldo

1965	*Selected Writings.* Edited and with a Foreword by William M. Gilman. New York: New American Library.

Galanter, Marc

1971	"Hinduism, Secularism and the Indian Judiciary." 21 *Philosophy East and West*, 467-87.
1972	"The Aborted Restoration of 'Indigenous' Law in India," *Comparative Studies in Society and History*, 14, 53-70.
1978	"Indian Law as an Indigenous Conceptual System," From Social Science Research Council, *ITEMS,* Vol. 32, Nos. 3-4, December 1978. pp. 42-46.
1981	"Justice in Many Rooms: Courts, Private Ordering and Indigenous Law," *Journal of Legal Pluralism*, pp. 1-47.

Galston, William A.

1980	*Justice and the Human Good.* Chicago: University of Chicago Press.

Gandhi, M. K.

1959[1947]	*India of My Dream.* Ahmedabad: Navajivan Publishing House.

Geertz, Clifford

1973	*The Interpretation of Cultures.* New York: Basic Books Inc.
1983	*Local Knowledge.* New York: Basic Books, Inc.

Hatch, Elvin

1983	*Culture and Morality, The Relativity of Values in Anthropology.* New York: Columbia University Press.

References

Holmes, Oliver Wendell
1960 "The Path of the Law." In *The American Pragmatists*. Eds. Milton R. Ronvitz and Gail Kennedy. New York: World Publishing Company.

Hsu, Francis L. K.
1963 *Clan, Caste, and Club*. Princeton: D. Van Nostrand Company, Inc.

James, William
1974 *Pragmatism*. New York: New American Library.

Joshi, P. C.
1979 "Gandhi and Nehru: The Challenge of a New Society." In *Gandhi and Nehru* (with B. R. Nanda and Raj Krishna). Delhi: Oxford University Press.

Khare, R. S.
1983 *Normative Culture and Kinship: Essays on Hindu Categories, Processes and Perspectives*. New Delhi: Vikas Publishing House.

1984 *The Untouchable As Himself*. New York: Cambridge University Press.

Kothari, Rajni
1970 *Politics in India*. Boston: Little Brown and Co.

Lévi-Strauss, C.
1966 *The Savage Mind*. Chicago: The University of Chicago Press.

Lukes, Steven
1973 *Individualism*. New York: Harper Torchbooks.

Madan, T. N.
1966 "For a Sociology of India," *In Contributions to Indian Sociology*, No. IX, 1-16.

Macpherson, C. B.
1972 *The Real World of Democracy*. New York: Oxford University Press.

1977 *The Life and Times of Liberal Democracy*. New York: Oxford University Press.

Merton, R. K.
1957 *Social Theory and Social Structure*. Glencoe: Free Press.

Mookerjee, Girija K.
1972 *Nehru The Humanist*. New Delhi: Trimurti Publications Private Limited.

Morris-Jones, W. H.
1971 *The Government and Politics of India.* London: Hutchinson University Library.

Nehru, Jawaharlal
1950 *Visit to America.* New York: The John Day Company.
1962 *"India Today and Tomorrow,"* [Maulana Azad Memorial Lectures.] in *India and the World.* Ed. by Humayun Kabir. New Delhi: Allied Publishers.
1981[1946] *The Discovery of India.* Oxford: The University Press.

Nisbet, Robert A.
1953 *The Quest for Community.* New York: Oxford University Press.

Putnam, Hilary
1981 *Reason, Truth and History.* Cambridge: University Press.

Saran, A. K.
1962 "Review of Contributions, No. IV," in *The Eastern Anthropologist,* Vol. XV, No. 1.

Schneider, David M.
1969 "Kinship, Nationality and Religion." In V. Turner, ed. *Forms of Symbolic Action. Proceedings of the 1969 annual spring meeting of the American Ethnological Society,* 116-25.
1976 "Notes Toward a Theory of Culture." In *Meaning in Anthropology.* Ed. K. Basso and H. Selby. Albuquerque: University of New Mexico Press.
1980 *American Kinship: A Cultural Account.* Chicago: The University of Chicago Press.

Schumpeter, Joseph
1947 *Capitalism, Socialism and Democracy.* (2nd Edition). New York: Oxford University Press.

Singer, Milton
1972 *When a Great Tradition Modernizes: An Anthropological Approach to Indian Civilization.* New York: Praeger.
1984 *Man's Glassy Essence.* Bloomington: Indiana University Press.

Srinivas, M. N.
1966 *Social Change in Modern India.* Berkeley: University of California Press.

Tagore, Rabindranath
1971[1922] *Creative Unity.* Calcutta: MacMillan and Company.

References

Thoreau, Henry David
1983[1854]   *Walden and Civil Disobedience.* With an Introduction by Michael Meyer. New York: Penguin Books.